WHITNEY MILLER'S
new southern table

MY FAVORITE FAMILY RECIPES WITH A MODERN TWIST

Whitney Miller

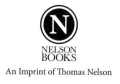

NELSON
BOOKS

An Imprint of Thomas Nelson

Published in Nashville, Tennessee, by Nelson Books, an imprint of Thomas Nelson. Nelson Books and Thomas Nelson are registered trademarks of HarperCollins Christian Publishing, Inc.

Photography by Justin Fox Burks

Thomas Nelson, Inc., titles may be purchased in bulk for educational, business, fund-raising, or sales promotional use. For information, please e-mail SpecialMarkets@ThomasNelson.com.

Library of Congress Cataloging-in-Publication Data

Miller, Whitney.
  Whitney Miller's new southern table : my favorite family recipes with a modern twist / Whitney Miller.
    pages cm
  ISBN 978-0-7180-1160-4
1. Cooking, American--Southern style. 2. Cooking--Southern States. I. Title. II. Title: New southern table.
  TX715.2.S68M555 2015
  641.5975--dc23   2015010774

Printed in the United States of America

15 16 17 18 19 QG 6 5 4 3 2 1

To my mom, Mary, thank you for having the patience to teach me how to cook at such a young age and for taking on so many roles—sous chef, traveling partner, editor, recipe tester, taster, and prop stylist. You helped me achieve my goals and dreams of becoming a chef and cookbook author. I could not have completed this cookbook without you. Love you!

Contents

Introduction

C ome on over; there's plenty!" "Pull up an extra chair!" "Set another place at the table!" These are familiar phrases that I've heard over the course of my life. In my South, there doesn't have to be an occasion or special event for an invitation to share a meal at the family table. Southern hospitality knows no season. Having grown up in a family where it was not unusual to have thirty to forty people for Sunday dinner, I learned at an early age how to cook enough to share.

Since the release of my first cookbook, *Modern Hospitality*, I have been blessed with opportunities to travel not only throughout the United States but internationally as well. I have shared my Southern family table in China, South Africa, and Malaysia. And I have learned that hospitality and fellowship over good food are enjoyed throughout the world.

My hospitality roots run deep. Having learned from my mom and great-grandmother Strahan how to cook for a few or a crowd, I often cook a large meat entrée such as a roast, pork loin, or whole chicken on the weekend, plenty for family as well as any unexpected guests. This simple act not only reconnects me to warm memories of the past, but also works well for modern times, allowing me to plan a week's menu in advance. Adding favorite vegetable side dishes from my roots brings to the table happy memories of my great-grandmother McCarter, a sure forerunner of the farm-to-table movement. One of my earliest mental pictures places her in the garden, head covered with

My great-grandmother Strahan and a spread of food she prepared.

a bonnet, hoe in hand, tilling the earth. Through stories told by my granny Christine, I learned that she grew up in a family that was mainly vegetarian, my great-grandma's garden serving as their greatest source of food. Her earthy and natural recipes included crusty slices of cornbread with churned butter, crispy fried okra slices, and homemade apple pies. Her love, shown through her homegrown foods, brought family together as nothing else could.

My great-grandmothers have inspired me in many ways. They grew up during the Great Depression and learned quickly how to stretch meals creatively and reduce waste. In Great-Grandma McCarter's kitchen, an apple from her tree, minus the thinnest peel, could become a mouthwatering dessert or an unexpected ingredient, adding natural tartness and contrast to her crispy coleslaw. Following their examples, I use my creativity to transform a weekend pork loin dish into weeknight meals of Pulled Pork Nachos and Southern Carnitas. While a slow-cooked pork loin could easily be dismissed as classic and traditional, my modern touches with unique spices and sauces make for an easy answer to the "What's for dinner?" question.

In this cookbook, you will find more recipes going back to my Southern roots. Preserving traditional family flavors, I also add my own special touches by lightening up classic dishes without losing flavor, experimenting with different Southern ingredients, and using new techniques and cooking methods I've learned over the years. You also will find new recipe creations incorporating Southern ingredients into dishes influenced by my travels over the past years. So get inspired to share your family table, try a new recipe, or put a modern touch on a traditional favorite, and then pull up a chair and enjoy.

My sister, cousin, and me with my great-grandmother and grandmother.

My Southern Pantry

O ne of my favorite challenges when I appeared on the television show *MasterChef* was the mystery box. The challenge of using a few random ingredients and creating a cohesive, delicious dish is thrilling. At times I have felt as though my pantry is a mystery box full of dry goods, cans, and spices ready to be whipped up into a meal. My well-stocked Southern pantry means I'm always prepared to create a dish or prepare a snack for unexpected guests.

Dry Goods

All-purpose flour

Self-rising flour

Self-rising cornmeal

Stone-ground cornmeal

Stone-ground grits

Light brown sugar

Pure cane sugar (white sugar)

Baking powder

Baking soda

Cornstarch

Panko bread crumbs

Powdered unflavored gelatin

Jasmine or long-grain white rice

Dried beans (red and large white limas)

Dried fruits (apples, peaches, and cranberries)

Nuts (pecans, pistachios, almonds, and peanuts)

Chocolate (semisweet, dark, milk, and white)

Cocoa (unsweetened and dark)

Sweetened shredded coconut
Pasta (spaghetti, gnocchi, shells, and acini di pepe)
Coffee beans and ground coffee

Tea (black and green)
Garlic
Yellow onions
Sweet potatoes

Canned Goods

Beans (black, lima, and butter)
Coconut milk

Tomatoes (whole, diced, paste, and sauce)
Chipotle peppers in adobo sauce

Spices and Herbs

Fine sea salt
Cracked black pepper
Garlic powder
Onion powder
Smoked paprika
Ground coriander
Ground cumin
Chili powder

Cayenne pepper
Dried dill
Dried parsley
Dried Italian seasoning
Crushed red pepper flakes
Cinnamon sticks
Ground cinnamon
Pure vanilla extract

Liquids

Extra-virgin olive oil
Vinegar (rice and balsamic)
Worcestershire sauce
Soy sauce
Dry white wine

Maple syrup (keep refrigerated after opening)
Honey
Stock (chicken and beef)
Broth (chicken)

Condiments

Mayonnaise
Natural peanut butter

Sriracha hot chili sauce
Stone-ground mustard

Breakfast

Whether you're preparing toast and preserves or biscuits and gravy, you're not just making breakfast, you're making memories. I didn't really realize this until I started thinking about favorite breakfast moments and foods. Of course, I thought about that surprise birthday breakfast in bed with my favorite foods, complete with a flower. And then there was the Christmas my whole family gathered in the kitchen to cook our favorite breakfast foods—pancakes with blueberry syrup, scrambled or fried eggs, grits, biscuits or toast, and gravy, a smorgasbord of sorts.

Olive Oil Biscuits (page 5)

Olive Oil Biscuits

|||||||||||||||||||||||||||||||||||||||||||||||||||||||||||||||||||||||||||||||||||||||||||||||||||||||||||||||||||||||||||||||||||||||||||||||||

Biscuits are the hallowed bread of the South, eaten for breakfast or dinner, even for dessert, savored with a slathering of fresh fruit preserves or cane syrup. Biscuit-making is an art, passed down through generations. I can still picture my great-grandmother Strahan's long fingers smoothly working the dough. With her many years of practice, fast work was made of the large mound of dough, resulting in large pans of biscuits, piled mile high and fluffy. Turning the biscuits in the oil in the pan and then patting their tops resulted in brown crusts that were a delicious contrast to the soft, fluffy insides. While my great-grandmother made and turned her biscuits using vegetable oil, I have updated and lightened up this Southern classic by substituting olive oil. Using the same large yellow Pyrex bowl that she used, I follow those time-honored steps, celebrating the achievement of that same light and fluffy texture that my great-grandmother's biscuits were famous for. I can still remember her words as they echoed around the table: "Don't just take one, have two. There are plenty more!"

1/4 cup plus 2 tablespoons extra-virgin olive oil, divided

2 cups self-rising flour, plus more for biscuit cutter

3/4 to 1 cup whole milk

Softened butter

Preheat the oven to 425 degrees F. Grease a 9-inch cast-iron skillet with 2 tablespoons olive oil.

Sift the flour into a medium bowl. Make a well in the center of the flour and pour 1/4 cup olive oil in the well. Using your hand, gently stir the olive oil into the flour until incorporated. Add the milk a little at a time while continuing to work the flour with your fingers. When a wet dough forms, begin using a down-across-up-and-over folding technique to incorporate the milk until a moist and sticky dough forms. If the dough is too wet, add 1 to 2 tablespoons more flour. Be careful not to overwork the dough.

Transfer the dough to a floured surface. Gently press the dough into a 1-inch-thick round.

Coat a 2½- to 3-inch round biscuit cutter in flour and cut out the biscuits, being sure to press straight down through the dough. Form the scraps of dough together and continue cutting. Place the biscuits close together in the greased skillet.

Bake the biscuits for about 12 minutes, until they have fully risen. Do not overcook. If the tops are still pale, change the oven setting to broil and broil until golden brown. Serve warm with butter.

◐ *Makes about 7 biscuits.*

Tomato Gravy

One of my fondest memories is of my grandpa Larry teaching me how to make tomato gravy; for him, it was the ideal meal! After my sister Brittyn and I spent the evening at his house, looking at old photographs and laughing at the memories, he announced that we were making tomato gravy and biscuits for dinner. The lesson began; I carefully listened and followed his directions to create first the brown roux and then the actual tomato gravy. The gravy was so good ladled over a hot, fluffy biscuit fresh from the oven. It soaked into the feathery softness of the biscuit, lending a creamy goodness to every bite. Keeping to the tradition of tomato gravy–making, I created my own version, enhancing the flavor with garlic and retaining the rich, creamy taste while losing much of the oil.

1/4 cup canola oil
1/3 cup self-rising or all-purpose flour
1/4 cup diced yellow onion
1 cup water

1 (28-ounce) can whole peeled tomatoes
1 clove garlic, minced
3/4 teaspoon fine sea salt

Heat the oil in a 12-inch cast-iron skillet over medium heat. Stir in the flour until smooth.

Increase the heat to medium-high and cook until the flour mixture turns dark brown, stirring constantly.

Reduce the heat to medium. Add the diced onion and water. Stir until combined. Drain the canned tomatoes, reserving 1/2 cup of the tomato juice. Add the reserved tomato juice, tomatoes, garlic, and salt to the skillet. Stir until combined. With the back of a spoon, press against the tomatoes to break them into pieces. Cook for about 20 minutes, stirring occasionally. Season with salt to taste. Serve warm with Olive Oil Biscuits (see recipe on page 5).

● *Makes 5 to 7 servings.*

Baked Donuts

||||||||||||||||||||||||||||||||||||||||||||||||||||||||||||||||||||||||||||||||||||||||||||||||||||||||||||||||||||||||||||||||

Who doesn't like donuts, especially when you have stacks of mini, bite-size donuts! When my mom was growing up and donut franchises were not so common, she cut canned biscuits into ring shapes and then fried them into tiny donuts to be glazed with a sugary coating or just tossed in a cinnamon and sugar mixture. My recipe takes a healthy twist by baking the donuts and incorporating vegetables into the batter.

1 3/4 cups all-purpose flour

2 teaspoons baking powder

1/2 teaspoon fine sea salt

1 1/2 teaspoons ground cinnamon, divided

1/2 teaspoon ground nutmeg

1/2 teaspoon ground allspice

1/3 cup canola oil

1/2 cup firmly packed light brown sugar

1 large egg

1 teaspoon pure vanilla extract

3/4 cup sweet potato, acorn squash, or pumpkin puree

1/4 cup nonfat milk

1/4 cup vanilla yogurt

3 tablespoons butter

1/2 cup pure cane sugar

Preheat the oven to 350 degrees F. Grease a nonstick mini donut pan with cooking spray.

Sift the flour, baking powder, salt, 1/2 teaspoon of the cinnamon, nutmeg, and allspice into a bowl.

In a large bowl whisk together the oil, brown sugar, egg, vanilla, sweet potato puree, milk, and yogurt until smooth. Stir the flour mixture into the sweet potato mixture until just combined.

Spoon the batter into a gallon-size zip-top freezer bag and seal the bag. Snip off a 1/2-inch tip from a bottom corner of the bag.

Squeeze the bag to pipe the batter into each section of the donut pan. Bake for 10 to 12 minutes, until a wooden pick inserted near the center comes out clean. Transfer the donuts to a baking sheet. Repeat with the rest of the batter. Let the baked donuts cool for a few minutes.

Melt the butter in a small bowl. Combine the sugar and remaining 1 teaspoon cinnamon in a zip-top plastic bag.

Dip the slightly warm donuts in the melted butter and toss them in the cinnamon-sugar mixture to coat. Serve immediately.

❯ *Makes 24 mini donuts.*

Griddled Blueberry Muffins

While at home in Poplarville, Mississippi, known as the Blueberry Capital of the state, I love to serve my family and guests homemade blueberry muffins, made from the fruit gathered from the blueberry bushes lining our driveway. First, I make the muffins, then I slice and griddle them on an iron skillet. My mother often told me about how her grandmother McCarter would do this to her biscuits, candying them with syrup. This cooking technique takes the muffins from a breakfast or brunch food and elevates them to dessert.

5 tablespoons butter, divided
1 1/2 cups all-purpose flour
1/4 teaspoon fine sea salt
1/2 teaspoon baking powder
1/2 teaspoon baking soda
1/8 teaspoon grated lemon zest
1/4 cup pure cane sugar
1/2 cup low-fat buttermilk

3 tablespoons whole milk
1 large egg
3 tablespoons honey
1 teaspoon pure vanilla extract
1 cup fresh blueberries
Coarse sugar sprinkles, optional
Powdered sugar, optional

Preheat the oven to 350 degrees F. Line a 6-cup jumbo muffin pan with paper liners.

In a medium microwave-safe bowl, melt 4 tablespoons of the butter and let cool slightly.

In a bowl stir together the flour, salt, baking powder, and baking soda.

Add the lemon zest, sugar, buttermilk, milk, egg, honey, and vanilla to the slightly cooled butter and whisk until combined. Using a rubber spatula, fold in half of the flour mixture. Do not overmix.

Add the blueberries to the remaining flour mixture and toss to coat. Fold the blueberries and flour mixture into the muffin batter.

Divide the batter evenly among the paper liners. Top each with the coarse sugar sprinkles, if using.

Bake the muffins for 18 to 22 minutes, until lightly browned. Let them cool for about 15 minutes. Cut the muffins in half.

Grease a cast-iron griddle with the remaining 1 tablespoon butter and heat over medium-high heat. Working in batches, place the muffin halves on the griddle and cook until toasted and browned, 30 seconds to 1 minute. Repeat with the remaining muffins. Serve immediately with butter and a sprinkling of powdered sugar, if using.

◉ *Makes 6 servings.*

Sweet Potato–Banana Nut Muffins

Use leftover baked sweet potato to add a naturally sweet, rich flavor to banana nut muffins. Serve with cinnamon butter to wake up your taste buds in the morning.

Muffins

4 1/2 tablespoons butter
1 3/4 cups all-purpose flour
1/4 teaspoon fine sea salt
3/4 teaspoon baking powder
3/4 teaspoon baking soda
1/8 teaspoon ground cinnamon
3/4 cup mashed baked sweet potato

2 small very ripe bananas
1/4 cup pure cane sugar
3/4 cup low-fat buttermilk
1/4 cup whole milk
1 large egg
3 tablespoons honey
1 teaspoon pure vanilla extract

Pecan Topping

1 tablespoon butter
1 tablespoon pure cane sugar

1/4 teaspoon ground cinnamon
3/4 cup chopped pecans

To prepare the muffins, preheat the oven to 350 degrees F. Line a 12-cup muffin pan with paper liners.

In a medium microwave-safe bowl, melt the butter and let cool slightly.

In a bowl stir together the flour, salt, baking powder, baking soda, and cinnamon.

Add the sweet potato and bananas to the slightly cooled butter and mash until smooth. Stir in the sugar, buttermilk, milk, egg, honey, and vanilla until incorporated. Using a rubber spatula, fold in the flour mixture, one-third at a time. Do not overmix. Divide the batter evenly among the paper liners.

To prepare the pecan topping, melt the butter in a small microwave-safe bowl. Add the sugar, cinnamon, and pecans. Stir until combined. Scatter the pecan topping evenly over the muffin batter.

Bake the muffins for 18 to 20 minutes. Let cool for 5 minutes. Serve warm.

Makes 12 muffins.

Peach Crumb Muffins

My grandfather, known affectionately as Daddy Bob, loved to tell a tale about some prized peaches. He also loved a good prank. His father-in-law, O.J., had a peach tree in his yard, and everyone knew not to pick his peaches! One Sunday after church Daddy Bob stopped by a fruit stand and hand-selected the exact number of peaches on O.J.'s tree and parceled them out to his daughters, instructing them to run in and exclaim to their papa O.J., "Look what we have!" Daddy Bob laughed as he shared, "You should have seen the horrified look on O.J.'s face!" He thought his precious little granddaughters had picked all his prized peaches. Needless to say, as soon as the tree was surveyed, the cat was out of the bag. Fresh peaches are still a family favorite, and whenever I serve my peach crumb muffins, our memories are stirred, and we all have a laugh.

Muffins

4 1/2 tablespoons butter

1 3/4 cups all-purpose flour

1/4 teaspoon fine sea salt

3/4 teaspoon baking powder

3/4 teaspoon baking soda

1/4 teaspoon ground cinnamon

1/4 cup pure cane sugar

3/4 cup low-fat buttermilk

1/4 cup whole milk

1 large egg

3 1/2 tablespoons honey

1 teaspoon pure vanilla extract

1 cup diced fresh peaches (or frozen and thawed)

Crumb Topping

3 tablespoons butter, cut into cubes

6 tablespoons all-purpose flour

1/3 cup firmly packed light brown sugar

1/8 teaspoon ground cinnamon

6 tablespoons chopped pecans

To make the muffins, preheat the oven to 350 degrees F. Line a 12-cup muffin pan with paper liners.

In a medium microwave-safe bowl, melt the butter and let cool slightly.

In another bowl stir together the flour, salt, baking powder, baking soda, and cinnamon.

Add the sugar, buttermilk, milk, egg, honey, and vanilla to the slightly cooled butter and whisk until combined.

Using a rubber spatula, fold half of the flour mixture into the milk mixture. Do not overmix.

Place the peaches in the bowl with the remaining flour mixture and toss to coat.

Fold the peaches and flour mixture into the batter. Divide the batter evenly among the paper liners.

To prepare the crumb topping, mix the butter into the flour with a fork until incorporated. Add the brown sugar, cinnamon, and pecans. Stir until combined. Scatter the topping evenly over the muffin batter.

Bake the muffins for 18 to 20 minutes. Let cool for 5 minutes. Serve warm.

◗ *Makes 12 muffins.*

My grandfather, Daddy Bob, and grandmother, Nanny Ida. This was the garden they planted year after year.

Cinnamon Cran-Raisin Bread

|||||||||||||||||||||||||||||||||||||||||||||||||||||||||||||||||||||||||||||||||||||||||||||||||||||||||||||||||||||||||||||||||||||||||||||||||||||||||||

Homemade bread. What more can I say? My mom is a bread lover. She claims that bread is her dessert. In this case I would agree. As this homemade bread bakes, the fragrant smell of the cinnamon draws you in; then the intense flavor of the cinnamon, contrasting with the sweet and tart cran-raisins, wins you over. Enjoy this bread warm or toasted with butter. It is also great for making homemade croutons or Cinnamon and Sugar Crisps.

1 (.25-ounce) envelope active dry yeast
2 tablespoons pure cane sugar
1/2 cup plus 1/3 cup lukewarm water
1/2 cup plus 1/3 cup warm whole milk, not over 110 degrees F
1/4 cup plus 1 tablespoon olive oil
4 cups bread flour, plus more for dusting

1/8 teaspoon grated orange zest
1 teaspoon fine sea salt
1/2 cup sweetened dried cranberries
1/2 cup raisins
1 large egg
1/2 cup firmly packed light brown sugar
2 tablespoons ground cinnamon

In the bowl of a stand mixer, combine the yeast, sugar, water, and milk. Let stand for 5 minutes. Add ¼ cup of the oil, flour, orange zest, and salt to the bowl. Using a paddle attachment, beat on medium speed until the dough is smooth. Add the cranberries and raisins. Replace the paddle with the dough hook and increase the speed to high. After 2 to 4 minutes the dough will become sticky and form a ball.

Place the dough in a lightly oiled bowl and turn to coat. Cover the dough with plastic wrap and let rise until doubled in size, about 1 hour.

In a small bowl beat the egg. In another small bowl mix the brown sugar and cinnamon.

Transfer the dough to a lightly floured surface and cut in half. Return half of the dough to the bowl. On the floured surface press the dough into an 8 x 10-inch rectangle. Brush the dough with some of the beaten egg and evenly cover it with half of the cinnamon-sugar mixture. Lightly press the mixture into the dough. Starting at the short end roll the dough up tightly, pinch the seams together to close, and tuck the ends under the log. Roll the dough back and forth to form a smooth cylinder. Repeat with the other half of the dough.

Transfer the dough loaves to a parchment paper–lined baking sheet, smooth side up. Cover the loaves with a tea towel and let rise for 1 hour.

Preheat the oven to 425 degrees F.

Bake the loaves for 15 minutes. Cover with a piece of parchment paper; reduce the temperature to 400 degrees F and bake for an additional 10 minutes. Transfer the loaves to a wire rack to cool.

Thinly slice and serve warm, or store in an airtight container for up to 1 week.

● *Makes 2 loaves.*

Quick-and-Easy Cinnamon Rolls

How easy is this? Use my Olive Oil Biscuit dough, and add cinnamon and sugar to the rolled-out dough to make these easy cinnamon rolls. Cooking them in a muffin tin helps them retain their shape. These are quick, perfect bites to share with family and friends.

Cinnamon Rolls

2 tablespoons extra-virgin olive oil, divided

Olive Oil Biscuit dough (page 5)

1/4 cup plus 2 tablespoons firmly packed light brown sugar, divided

1/2 teaspoon ground cinnamon, divided

1/3 cup chopped pecans

Glaze

5 to 6 tablespoons powdered sugar

1 tablespoon whole milk

To make the cinnamon rolls, preheat the oven to 375 degrees F. Grease 9 cups of a muffin pan with 1 tablespoon of the olive oil.

Place the dough on a floured surface. Using floured hands, gently press the dough out into a rectangle about ¼ inch thick. If the dough is too sticky to press out, gently fold in a little flour. Brush the remaining 1 tablespoon olive oil over the dough.

In a small bowl combine ¼ cup of the brown sugar with ¼ teaspoon of the cinnamon. Sprinkle evenly over the dough. Starting at one of the long sides, roll the dough into a cylinder. Cut the cylinder into 9 equal pieces.

In a small bowl combine the remaining 2 tablespoons brown sugar and remaining ¼ teaspoon cinnamon. Stir in the chopped pecans. Divide the mixture evenly among the greased muffin cups. Lightly press the pieces of dough on top of the pecan mixture in the muffin cups.

Bake for 18 minutes or until lightly golden brown.

While the cinnamon rolls are baking, prepare the glaze. Combine the powdered sugar and milk until thick and smooth.

Let the cinnamon rolls cool for 5 minutes, drizzle the glaze over them, and then transfer to a serving platter. Serve warm.

● *Makes 9 cinnamon rolls.*

Gluten-Free Skillet Toast

It seems that a lot of people—my dad included—are going gluten-free for various health reasons. Making the switch to gluten-free bread has meant an adjustment in texture. Trying a different technique, I cooked my dad's toast in a skillet rather than using his usual under-the-broiler method. The result was toast with a wonderful buttery flavor, a softer interior, and a perfect crunchy exterior. This new Skillet Toast goes perfectly with my Blackberry Refrigerator Preserves or Strawberry Refrigerator Preserves (see recipes on pages 21 and 22).

1 tablespoon butter

4 slices gluten-free sandwich bread

Heat an 8-inch cast-iron skillet or nonstick sauté pan over medium-high heat. Melt a sliver of butter in the pan. Lay the bread on top and cook until toasted, about 30 seconds. Lift the slice of bread with a spatula and add another sliver of butter. Flip the bread and cook until the second side is toasted, about 30 seconds. Wipe the skillet clean and repeat with the remaining butter and bread slices. If the pan becomes too hot while cooking, decrease the heat slightly.

Makes 4 pieces of toast.

Note: I prefer to use Udi's gluten-free white sandwich bread.

Gluten-Free White Squash Bread

This recipe grew out of an abundance of white squash. My dad planted a small garden, consisting mainly of corn, tomatoes, peppers, and squash. It seemed that the white patty pan squash would never stop producing. My family and I ate them every way we could think of—roasted, fried, etc. Then I got creative, and my white squash bread was the delicious result. Although zucchini is the squash usually associated with bread-making, the white squash makes a great substitute.

1/4 cup coconut oil
2 tablespoons butter
4 large eggs
1/4 cup pure cane sugar
1/4 cup firmly packed dark brown sugar
1/4 cup honey
1 teaspoon pure vanilla extract
1 1/2 cups brown rice flour

1/2 cup oat flour
1 teaspoon baking soda
1 teaspoon ground cinnamon
1/4 teaspoon grated orange zest
1/2 cup chopped pecans
3/4 cup grated white scalloped squash (patty pan squash)
1/4 cup grated pear
Old-fashioned oats, optional

Preheat the oven to 350 degrees F. Grease an 8½ x 4½-inch glass loaf pan.

Melt the coconut oil and butter in a small saucepan over medium heat. Let cool slightly.

Whisk the eggs in a large bowl until light and fluffy. Add the cane sugar, brown sugar, honey, and vanilla. Gradually whisk in the melted coconut oil and butter until combined.

In a bowl stir together the rice flour, oat flour, baking soda, cinnamon, orange zest, and pecans. Stir into the egg mixture.

Place the grated squash and pear on a stack of paper towels and press to extract as much liquid as possible. Fold into the batter.

Pour the batter into the prepared pan. Sprinkle a few oats on top of the batter, if using. Bake for 45 to 48 minutes on the middle rack of the oven. Transfer to a wire rack and let cool for 10 minutes. Remove the bread from the pan and return to the rack to cool completely.

◐ *Makes 1 loaf.*

Notes: If you don't want to make the bread gluten-free, substitute all-purpose flour for the brown rice flour. For oat flour, pulse gluten-free old-fashioned oats in a spice grinder or food processor until a powder forms. If you can't find patty pan squash, zucchini can be substituted.

Blackberry Refrigerator Preserves

Spring and summer are wonderful times for a kid in Mississippi. An afternoon walk can become an adventure resulting in a pocketful of marble-size sweet blueberries and bright red plums or even a handful of big, juicy blackberries. I have risked a few briars and experienced many a thorn for the pleasure of picking enough blackberries for Great-Grandma McCarter to make jelly or preserves. Drawing on those memories, I developed my recipe for easy refrigerator preserves. The vibrant color, so purple it's almost black, hints at the rich, slightly tart taste. When the dark richness of the blackberry preserves mixes with the buttery taste of crisp toast, only the addition of a cold glass of milk can make it better.

2 cups fresh blackberries (or frozen and thawed)
1/4 cup white grape juice
1/4 cup 100 percent pear juice

1 teaspoon fresh lemon juice
7 tablespoons honey
1 tablespoon plus 3/4 teaspoon Sure-Jell No Sugar Needed Fruit Pectin

Combine the blackberries, grape juice, pear juice, lemon juice, and honey in a medium saucepan. Stir well. If using fresh blackberries, cook over medium-high heat for 2 minutes to release the blackberry juices. Whisk in the Sure-Jell.

Bring the mixture to a boil over high heat and cook for 2 minutes, stirring constantly. Remove the pan from the heat and spoon the preserves into 2 clean 1/2-pint jars and halfway up another clean 1/2-pint jar. Secure with lids. Let cool to room temperature. Store the preserves in the refrigerator for up to 2 weeks.

◐ *Makes 1 1/2 pints.*

Strawberry Refrigerator Preserves

Plant City, Florida, is the home of the Strawberry Festival as well as many strawberry farms. For a strawberry lover like me, visiting was pure heaven. During the festival I tasted strawberry cookies, strawberry milkshakes, and the area's famous strawberry shortcakes. Returning home with strawberry fever, I got to work creating my recipe for fresh and easy strawberry preserves. Light in sugar, these preserves have a remarkable fresh strawberry taste. Divine on toast or with biscuits, the preserves are light enough to serve with dessert; just don't forget the homemade whipped cream.

2 cups chopped fresh strawberries (1/2-inch pieces)
1/2 cup white grape juice
1/2 cup 100 percent pear juice
1 teaspoon fresh lemon juice
4 tablespoons honey
1 tablespoon plus 3/4 teaspoon Sure-Jell No Sugar Needed Fruit Pectin

Combine the strawberries, grape juice, pear juice, lemon juice, and honey in a medium saucepan. Stir well. Cook over medium-high heat for 2 minutes, stirring occasionally. Whisk in the Sure-Jell.

Bring the mixture to a boil over high heat and cook for 2 minutes, stirring constantly. Remove the pan from the heat and spoon off any foam from the top. Spoon the preserves into 2 clean 1/2-pint jars. Secure with lids. Let cool to room temperature. Store the preserves in the refrigerator for up to 2 weeks.

◐ *Makes 1 pint.*

Persimmon Butter

The rich, complex flavors of my Persimmon Butter can be enjoyed by the spoonful, or as a spread for buttery biscuits or bread. If you don't have a persimmon tree near your house as I do, you can buy them at your local grocery or an Asian market.

4 large very ripe persimmons
1/2 cup pure maple syrup
3 tablespoons fresh orange juice

1/2 teaspoon vanilla bean paste or vanilla bean seeds
1/8 teaspoon ground cinnamon

Wash and cut off the green tops of the persimmons. Place a wire mesh strainer over a 4-cup measuring cup. Press each persimmon against the strainer to release the pulp. Discard seeds and skin. Repeat with the remaining persimmons to create about 2 cups of pulp.

Combine the persimmon pulp, maple syrup, orange juice, vanilla bean paste, and cinnamon in a small saucepan. Cook over medium to medium-high heat for 5 minutes, stirring constantly. Reduce the heat to medium-low and cook for 45 minutes, stirring occasionally. Increase the heat to medium to medium-high and cook for 1 minute, stirring constantly. Let cool slightly, then transfer the mixture to the bowl of a food processor. Pulse until the mixture is smooth. Transfer to a 16-ounce glass jar with a lid. Let cool completely. Use immediately or refrigerate for up to 1 week.

◗ *Makes about 2 cups.*

Note: I prefer to use Hachiya persimmons.

Breakfast Toast

Handheld breakfast items always go over well at my busy house. Prepare the aioli and boil the eggs the day before for easy assembly the next morning.

4 (1/2-inch thick) rustic bread slices

4 tablespoons Yogurt Aioli (see recipe on page 289)

1/2 cup packed fresh spinach

4 slices prosciutto or thinly sliced smoked ham

1 1/2 tablespoons julienne-cut sun-dried tomatoes in olive oil, drained

2 hard-boiled eggs, peeled and cut into 1/8-inch-thick slices

1 teaspoon finely chopped fresh chives

Preheat the broiler on high.

Place the bread slices on a baking sheet and broil until lightly browned and toasted; watch closely so that the bread does not burn.

Remove the pan from the oven and let the toast cool for a couple of minutes.

Spread a tablespoon of Yogurt Aioli on each piece of toast. Add a few pieces of spinach and top with a slice of prosciutto. Divide the sun-dried tomato strips among the toast and top each with a few slices of boiled egg. Sprinkle each with 1/4 teaspoon chives and serve immediately.

> *Makes 4 servings.*

Stacked Buttermilk Pancakes with Blueberry Syrup

Breakfast is special in my family, like a holiday sort of special. We all have our favorite breakfast items. One of my dad's favorites is pancakes with blueberry syrup. The pancakes are small and stacked, with a generous helping of warm blueberry syrup.

Pancakes

1 cup all-purpose flour

3/4 teaspoon baking powder

3/4 teaspoon baking soda

1/8 teaspoon fine sea salt

1 large egg

3 tablespoons pure cane sugar

3/4 cup low-fat buttermilk

3 tablespoons canola oil

1/2 teaspoon pure vanilla extract

2 tablespoons butter, or as much as you need to grease the griddle

Blueberry Syrup

2 cups maple syrup

1 1/2 cups fresh blueberries (or frozen and thawed)

To make the pancakes, sift the flour, baking powder, baking soda, and salt into a bowl.

In a medium bowl, whisk the egg, then add the sugar, buttermilk, oil, and vanilla. Whisk until combined. Whisk in the flour mixture until smooth. Let the batter rest for 5 minutes.

Heat a cast-iron griddle over medium-high heat. Grease the griddle with some of the butter. For mini pancakes drop the batter by tablespoonsful onto the griddle. For larger pancakes drop the batter by 2 to 3 tablespoonsful onto the griddle. Use the back of the spoon to spread the batter into a round. You should be able to fit 3 pancakes on the griddle at a time. Cook until bubbles form on top of the batter, 1 to 2 minutes. Flip the pancakes and cook for about 1 minute on the other side. If the pancakes brown too quickly, reduce the heat to medium. Transfer the pancakes to a serving plate. Grease the griddle again and repeat the process with the remaining batter.

To make the blueberry syrup, combine the syrup and blueberries in a microwave-safe bowl. Microwave for 1 to 1 1/2 minutes, until the syrup is warm and the blueberries are softened.

To serve, stack the warm pancakes on top of one another and serve with the warm blueberry syrup.

◐ *Makes 4 servings.*

Alternate Cooking Method: For baked pancakes, preheat the oven to 375 degrees F. Grease a 12-cup muffin pan with cooking spray. Drop 1 tablespoon of batter into each cup. Bake for 6 to 8 minutes, until the bottoms are golden brown and the pancakes release from the pan easily.

Cinnamon-Pecan Granola Bars

||||||||||||||||||||||||||||||||||||||||||||||||||||||||||||||||||||||||||||||||||||||||||||||||||||||||||||||||||||||||||||||||||||||||||||||||||||||||||||||||||||||||||||||

After mastering homemade granola, I decided to try my hand at making granola bars. It seemed like a daunting task, but after making my first batch, I realized that it wasn't much harder than making granola. What I love about these bars is the chewy *and* crunchy texture combination.

1 1/2 cups old-fashioned oats, divided

3 tablespoons raw, shelled pistachios

1/3 cup chopped pecans

2 tablespoons butter

1/3 cup honey

2 tablespoons light brown sugar

1 1/2 teaspoons pure vanilla extract

Pinch of fine sea salt

1/4 teaspoon ground cinnamon

Preheat the oven to 350 degrees F. Grease a 12-cup mini tart pan or mini muffin pan.

Place 1/2 cup of the oats in the bowl of a spice grinder or food processor and pulse until a powder forms. Pour the powder into a large bowl.

Place another 1/2 cup of the oats in the spice grinder and pulse a couple of times until the oats are coarsely chopped. Pour into the bowl with the powdered oats. Add the remaining 1/2 cup oats to the bowl.

Place the pistachios in the grinder and pulse until a powder forms. Pour into the bowl with the oats. Add the pecans and whisk until well combined.

In a small microwave-safe bowl, melt the butter. Add the honey and brown sugar and cook in 30-second intervals until the sugar has melted, stirring occasionally. Add the vanilla, salt, and cinnamon and mix well. Mix the butter mixture into the oat mixture. Divide the mixture evenly among the tart pans or muffin cups. Press with the back of a spoon until the mixture becomes compact.

Bake for 12 to 15 minutes, until set and golden brown. Let cool for 5 minutes, then transfer the granola bars to a wire rack to cool.

◉ *Makes 12 granola bars.*

Egg-in-a-Tortilla

Believe or not, I had never had "egg-in-a-hole" toast until I visited my uncle Dwight on a family vacation to Maryland. For breakfast one morning he showed me how to cut the bread slice and cook the egg in the middle. It was so simple and good! Using this as an inspiration and combining the idea with my love of Mexican food, I substituted a tortilla for the bread and created a new breakfast dish everyone in my house loves, especially when served with my Southern Verde Sauce.

4 small white corn tortillas
1 tablespoon butter, divided
4 large eggs
1/4 teaspoon fine sea salt

1/2 cup Southern Verde Sauce (see recipe on page 285)
Crumbled cotija cheese for garnish
Fresh cilantro leaves for garnish

Using a 2 1/4-inch round cutter, cut a hole in the middle of each tortilla.

Melt a fourth of the butter in a small sauté pan over medium-high heat. Add a tortilla and cook for 1 minute. Reduce the heat to medium. Crack an egg in a small bowl, then gently slip it onto the middle of the tortilla so that the yolk fits in the hole. Sprinkle a pinch of salt over the egg. Cover and cook for 2 minutes. Carefully flip the tortilla and cook for a few seconds. Transfer to a plate. Repeat the process with the remaining butter, tortillas, and eggs. Serve each egg-in-a-tortilla with 2 tablespoons Southern Verde Sauce, cotija cheese, and cilantro leaves.

● *Makes 4 servings.*

Note: If you can't find cotija, feta cheese can be substituted.

Sausage and Egg Pie

Eggs at my house are fresh and plentiful with my dad's henhouse of pet chickens, so I am able to experiment with lots of new egg recipes. Here is one of my family's favorites. The fresh tomatoes, creamy egg, savory sausage, and a surprise layer of Southern stone-ground grits make this a delicious all-in-one dish that is perfect for serving family and impressing company.

1 cup water
1/2 cup plus 2 tablespoons half-and-half, divided
2 tablespoons butter
1/2 teaspoon fine sea salt, divided
1/2 cup stone-ground grits
8 ounces bulk pork breakfast sausage

5 cups packed fresh baby spinach, stems removed
8 grape tomatoes, cut into halves
3/4 cup shredded sharp Cheddar cheese
6 large eggs
1/8 teaspoon cracked black pepper

Preheat the oven to 350 degrees F. Grease a 9½-inch deep-dish pie pan.

Combine the water and ½ cup of the half-and-half in a medium saucepan and bring to a low boil over medium-high heat. Add the butter and ¼ teaspoon salt. Stir until the butter is melted. Stir in the grits. Reduce the heat to medium-low. Cover and cook for 15 minutes, stirring occasionally. Evenly spread the grits mixture in the prepared pan.

In a medium sauté pan cook the sausage over medium-high heat until brown and no pink remains, breaking it up with a spoon as it cooks. Transfer the sausage to a paper towel-lined plate to drain.

Remove all but ½ teaspoon of the grease from the pan. Add the spinach to the pan and cook until wilted, 3 to 4 minutes. Season the spinach with a pinch of salt.

Crumble the sausage over the grits, then layer on the spinach, tomato halves, and cheese.

In a bowl whisk the eggs, remaining 2 tablespoons half-and-half, remaining ¼ teaspoon salt, and pepper until combined. Pour over the layered ingredients.

Bake for about 30 minutes, until set. Let stand for 5 minutes before serving.

◉ *Makes 6 to 8 servings.*

Note: Quick grits can be substituted to save time. Follow the directions on the box for cooking time.

Mock Mimosa

The Mimosa is the quintessential celebratory breakfast drink, usually composed of orange juice and champagne (or a sparkling wine). My Mock Mimosa gets its natural sweetness and a slightly tropical flair from the addition of pineapple juice and substitutes sparkling water for sparkling wine.

3 cups 100 percent orange juice
   (not from concentrate), chilled
3/4 cup 100 percent pineapple juice
   (not from concentrate), chilled

3/4 cup sparkling water, chilled
1 cup frozen pineapple chunks, optional

Combine the orange juice, pineapple juice, and sparkling water in a glass pitcher. Stir to blend well. To keep chilled, add the frozen pineapple chunks to the pitcher, if using. Serve cold.

● *Makes 6 servings.*

Mini Quiches

While visiting my sister Leslie, my mom created this quick and easy egg dish as the perfect breakfast for kids and moms on the go. The mini version was the perfect size for my nephew John Michael's small fingers (not yet fully adept at using a fork). The gluten-free bread round acts as a base instead of the traditional crust. Tiny diced vegetables are used as toppings and can vary according to taste.

Butter for greasing pan

12 slices gluten-free bread, cut into 2-inch rounds

4 slices bacon, crisply cooked and finely chopped

2 tablespoons finely chopped yellow onion

2 tablespoons finely chopped baby bella mushrooms

4 teaspoons finely chopped green bell pepper

1/2 cup shredded sharp Cheddar cheese

8 large eggs

4 tablespoons whole milk

1/4 teaspoon fine sea salt

1/4 teaspoon cracked black pepper

Preheat the oven to 350 degrees F. Grease a 12-cup muffin pan with butter.

Place a bread round in each muffin cup. Divide the bacon, onion, mushrooms, and green pepper evenly among the muffin cups. Top the vegetables with the cheese.

In a bowl whisk the eggs, milk, salt, and pepper until combined. Divide the egg mixture evenly among the muffin cups.

Bake for 9 to 10 minutes, until set. Let cool for 2 minutes and then transfer the mini quiches to a serving plate. Serve immediately.

● *Makes 12 mini quiches.*

Note: If you don't want to make the quiches gluten-free, a loaf of hearty multigrain bread can be substituted.

Socials
and Snacks

"...Practice hospitality."
—ROMANS 12:13

Southern hospitality: it's what we are known for; it has no season. My grandpa Larry spent a lot of time sitting on his front porch in the white wicker rocker. "Sit down awhile. I'll put a pot of coffee on or make some tea. Do you want something to eat? A cookie, piece of cake, or even a hot biscuit?" This is what my grandpa Larry was known for, how people remember him. He was carrying on the family tradition that Great-Grandma Strahan was famous for. She invited everyone she met to her house and offered whatever she had on hand. She did not stand on ceremony. It didn't have to be a special occasion or event. Enjoy entertaining, and make hospitality a practice in your home. The Mississippi Cheese Board is always a crowd-pleasing appetizer, whether for family or friends. Try your own variations on the Spicy Pimento Cheese, Southern "Fried" Pecans, and Pecan "Biscuit" Crackers. With a pantry full of basic ingredients and a little creativity, you're always ready for guests.

Buttermilk Ricotta Cheese

Mississippi Cheese Board

Cinnamon and Sugar Crisps

Buttermilk Scones with Yogurt Cream

Campfire S'mores Scones

Stuffed White Squash Dip with Baked Pita Chips

Tea Cake Biscotti

Chocolate Oat Crisps with Goat Cheese and Strawberries

Pecan "Biscuit" Crackers

Southern "Fried" Pecans

Zucchini and Squash Pickles

Crispy Green Tomato Corncakes with Spicy Pimento Cheese

PB&J Chicken Satays

Pulled Pork Nachos

Venison Egg Rolls with Sweet and Spicy Blackberry Sauce

Szechuan Chicken Wings with Cilantro Yogurt Dip

Deviled Eggs

Pork "Wings" with Buttermilk–Blue Cheese Dip

Coffee Milk Tea

Coconut Milk Tea

Sparkling Lemon-Limeade

Buttermilk Ricotta Cheese

IIIIIIIIIIIIIIIIIIIIIIIIIIIIIIIIIIIIIIIIIIIIIIIIIIIIIIIIIIIIIIIIIIIIIIIIIIIIIIIIIIIIIIIIIIIIIIIIIIIIIIIIIIIIIIIIIIIIIIIIIIIIIIIIIIIIIIIIIIIIIIIIIIIIIII

Living in a time of great self-sufficiency, my great-grandma McCarter not only grew her own vegetables and fruits, but also raised chickens for eggs and a cow for milk. My mom recalls that when she was little, her grandma always had fresh-churned butter and buttermilk in her icebox. A plate of hot crusty cornbread, dish of homemade butter, and glass of cold milk were sometimes the only dishes on her supper table. However, the freshness and flavor of these dairy products transformed the simplest of meals into a gourmet's delight. Yearning for that taste of homemade, I visited a local dairy to buy fresh milk and researched and experimented to make my own ricotta cheese. Although it doesn't take long to make, I learned the hard way to give my full attention to the process, giving it a loving hand and a light touch of heat. The result is an incredibly soft, pillowy cheese, great as a spread on crostini or as an important ingredient in my Seasonal Arugula Salad (page 94). I think my great-grandma would be proud.

4 cups good-quality whole milk   1/4 teaspoon fine sea salt
1 cup buttermilk

Combine the milk and buttermilk in a medium saucepan over medium-high heat. Bring to a low boil, stirring constantly with a wooden spoon. Reduce the heat to medium and cook until the curds separate from the whey, 10 to 15 minutes, gently stirring constantly. Remove the pan from the heat.

Line a large sieve with cheesecloth and place it over a deep bowl. Pour the milk mixture through, trapping the curds in the cheesecloth. Gently fold the salt into the curds. Let the cheese drain for 15 minutes. Bring the cheesecloth around the curds to form a ball and extract some of the liquid by gently squeezing. Discard the liquid.

Serve the ricotta cheese at room temperature or store in an airtight container in the refrigerator for up to 3 days.

⊙ *Makes one ricotta cheese ball.*

Mississippi Cheese Board

When I was selected as the first Southern chef to be featured at Chefdance, a five-night exclusive dinner event during the Sundance Film Festival in Park City, Utah, I not only wanted to share the flavors of the South but also wanted guests to experience an evening of Southern hospitality. My Mississippi Cheese Board, composed of toasted pecans for nibbling; homemade Buttermilk Ricotta Cheese served with Cinnamon and Sugar Crisps; grilled seasonal figs and peaches; and Southern honey for drizzling, was the perfect way to start the evening.

1 Buttermilk Ricotta Cheese ball (see recipe on page 43)
1 large firm, ripe peach
8 ripe figs

1 tablespoon butter, melted
1/4 cup chopped pecans
Pinch of fine sea salt
1/2 cup honey

Place the Buttermilk Ricotta Cheese ball on a serving tray and let stand at room temperature for about 15 minutes before serving.

Cut the peach into halves, discard the pit, and cut into 1/2-inch-thick slices. Cut the figs into about 1/4-inch-thick slices. Transfer half of the peach and fig slices to the serving tray.

Heat a grill pan over medium heat. Brush half of the butter on the pan. When the butter is hot and bubbling, add the peach slices in a single layer. Cook until grill marks appear, 3 to 4 minutes. Flip and cook for another 2 to 3 minutes. Transfer to the serving tray.

Brush the remaining butter on the pan. Add the fig slices and cook until grill marks appear, about 2 minutes on each side. Transfer to the serving tray.

Place the chopped pecans in a medium sauté pan over medium-low heat. Cook until toasted, 4 to 5 minutes, stirring frequently. Season the pecans with a pinch of salt and place in a small dish on the serving tray. Place the honey in a small bowl.

Serve the cheese, fruit, pecans, and honey with Cinnamon and Sugar Crisps (see recipe on page 46).

● *Makes 6 servings.*

Cinnamon and Sugar Crisps

Everyone loves cinnamon and sugar. These crisps are an easy addition to any cheese board or can be served alone as a sweet and crunchy treat. They are so simple to make by thinly slicing Cinnamon Cran-Raisin Bread, sprinkling with sugar, and toasting until crisp. Serve with homemade Buttermilk Ricotta Cheese (page 43), a slice of your favorite grilled fruit, and a drizzle of honey for a perfect accompaniment.

1 loaf Cinnamon Cran-Raisin Bread
   (see recipe on page 15)

2 tablespoons butter
2 tablespoons pure cane sugar

Preheat the oven to 375 degrees F. Line a rimmed baking sheet with parchment paper.

Using a serrated bread knife cut the bread diagonally into thin slices. Transfer to the baking sheet.

In a microwave-safe bowl melt the butter. Lightly brush the tops of the slices with the melted butter and sprinkle with the sugar.

Bake for 10 minutes or until lightly golden brown and crisp. Transfer to a wire rack and let cool completely.

Store the crisps in an airtight container for up to 1 week.

◗ *Makes about 30 crisps.*

Buttermilk Scones with Yogurt Cream

I was first introduced to light and flaky scones, served with creamy, slightly tart clotted cream and sweet jam, by a chef friend, Reza, better known as the Spice King, whom I met at a food show in Cape Town, South Africa. I instantly fell in love with the delectable taste of the scones as well as the hospitality of teatime. After learning that scone-making was as much a passed-down tradition as biscuit-making is in the Southern United States, I was eager to create and share my newfound hospitality offerings. You'll love not only the simplicity of this recipe but also its taste and versatility.

Yogurt Cream

1 cup whipping cream

1/4 cup Greek yogurt

Buttermilk Scones

Cooking spray

1 2/3 cups self-rising flour

Pinch of fine sea salt

1/3 cup cold butter, cut into cubes

2 1/2 tablespoons pure cane sugar

2 large eggs, divided

4 tablespoons buttermilk

Butter for serving

Jam for serving

To make the cream, pour the whipping cream into a deep bowl. Using an electric hand mixer, beat until soft peaks form. Fold in the yogurt until blended. Use immediately or store in an airtight container in the refrigerator for up to 1 day.

To make the scones, preheat the oven to 425 degrees F. Coat a baking sheet with cooking spray.

Sift the flour and salt into a large bowl. Add the butter and cut it into the flour with a fork until the mixture resembles coarse crumbs. Stir in the sugar.

In a bowl, beat 1 egg and the buttermilk until combined. Stir the egg mixture into the flour mixture until just incorporated. Using your hands, lightly knead the mixture to form a soft dough.

Place the dough on a lightly floured surface and shape into a ball. Pat the dough into about a 3/4- to 1-inch-thick round. Using a floured 2-inch cutter, quickly push the cutter down through the dough and lift without twisting. Place the scones on the prepared pan. Reshape the dough and repeat until all the dough has been used.

Beat the remaining egg in a bowl. Brush the tops of the scones with the beaten egg. Bake the scones for about 7 minutes. Transfer them immediately to a wire rack to cool.

Serve warm with the Yogurt Cream, butter, and jam.

◉ *Makes about 14 scones and 1 cup of Yogurt Cream.*

Campfire S'mores Scones

Joining the long line at a small coffee shop in California serving Intelligentsia coffee and pastries, I waited for a taste of what some say is the best coffee. Arriving at the front of the line, I ordered a latte and a s'mores scone. The coffee was really good, but the accompanying scone was amazing. The texture was crumbly, soft, and deliciously moist, with chunks of chocolate and a sticky maple marshmallow topping. As soon as I got home, I experimented with ingredients to create my own S'mores Scone recipe. They taste like a more decadent version of everyone's campfire favorite and are sure to impress family and friends.

Scones

Cooking spray
About 8 graham crackers
1 cup self-rising flour
1/4 teaspoon baking powder
1/8 teaspoon baking soda
Pinch of fine sea salt

1/3 cup cold butter, cut into cubes
2 1/2 tablespoons firmly packed light brown sugar
2 large eggs, divided
4 tablespoons buttermilk
1/3 cup semisweet chocolate chips

Maple Marshmallow Topping

1/4 cup cold water
1 (1/4-ounce) envelope unflavored gelatin

1/4 cup plus 2 tablespoons pure maple syrup

To make the scones, preheat the oven to 425 degrees F. Grease a baking sheet with cooking spray.

Place the graham crackers in a spice grinder or the bowl of a food processor and process until a powder forms. You'll need 2/3 cup. Pour the graham flour into a large bowl. Sift the flour, baking powder, baking soda, and salt over the graham flour.

Add the butter and cut it into the flour mixture with a fork until the mixture resembles coarse crumbs. Stir in the brown sugar.

In a bowl beat 1 egg and the buttermilk until blended. Stir into the flour mixture and mix until just incorporated. Stir in the chocolate chips. Using your hands, lightly knead the mixture to form a soft, slightly sticky dough.

Place the dough on a lightly floured surface and shape into a ball. Pat the dough into a 3/4- to 1-inch-thick round. Using a floured 2-inch cutter, quickly push the cutter down through the dough and lift without twisting. Place the scones on the prepared pan. Reshape the dough and repeat until all the dough has been used.

Beat the remaining egg in a bowl. Brush the tops of the scones with the beaten egg. Bake the scones for 7 minutes. Transfer them immediately to a wire rack to cool.

Make the Maple Marshmallow Topping while the scones are baking and cooling. Pour the water into a small saucepan. Sprinkle the gelatin over the water and cook over low heat until the gelatin has dissolved, stirring constantly. Add the maple syrup and stir until combined. Increase the heat to medium-high and cook until the mixture almost comes to a boil. Pour the warm syrup into a deep mixing bowl. Using an electric hand mixer beat on high speed for about 12 minutes or until doubled in volume and soft peaks form.

Once the scones have cooled, spoon a dollop of Maple Marshmallow Topping on top of each. Using a hand torch, toast each marshmallow-topped scone until browned. If you do not have a hand torch, heat the broiler and broil the scones until browned. Serve slightly warm.

● *Makes about 12 scones.*

Stuffed White Squash Dip with Baked Pita Chips

An underused vegetable, white squash suddenly became a major component in my cooking when our farm garden produced an extreme abundance. When roasted, the squash offers not only its delicious pulp but also a firm outer skin that serves as a natural container for this creamy dip. Sautéed onions add an extra level of flavor when added to the mixture.

Baked Pita Chips

3 pita bread rounds
3 tablespoons extra-virgin olive oil

1/4 teaspoon fine sea salt

Squash Dip

3 medium white scalloped squash
  (patty pan squash)
2 tablespoons plus 3 teaspoons extra-
  virgin olive oil, divided
2 tablespoons finely chopped yellow
  onion
1 clove garlic, minced
4 ounces cream cheese, softened

1/4 cup mayonnaise
1/4 teaspoon Worcestershire sauce
1/4 teaspoon fresh lemon juice
3 tablespoons grated Parmesan cheese
1/4 cup shredded pepper jack cheese
Pinch of cayenne pepper
Fine sea salt, to taste
2 tablespoons panko bread crumbs

To make the pita chips, preheat the oven to 375 degrees F.

Cut each pita into 8 wedges. Place on a baking sheet. Drizzle the olive oil over the

wedges. Sprinkle with the salt. Bake for 10 to 12 minutes, until toasted and golden brown. Store in an airtight container. To serve, rewarm the chips in a 250-degree oven for 5 minutes.

To make the squash dip, preheat the oven to 350 degrees F.

Place the squash on a baking sheet and brush 2 tablespoons of the olive oil over them. Bake for 30 to 35 minutes, until soft to the touch. Let cool slightly and then cut off the tops of each squash. Scoop out the seeds from all 3 squash and discard. Scrape the pulp from one of the squash and transfer to a wire mesh strainer over a bowl. Discard the shell. Carefully scoop out the pulp from the remaining 2 squash, leaving enough pulp for the squash to hold their shapes. Transfer the pulp to the strainer. Reserve both squash shells for stuffing.

Slightly press against the pulp in the strainer to remove excess liquid. Transfer to a bowl and mash with the back of a spoon.

Add 1 teaspoon of the olive oil to a small sauté pan and heat over medium heat. Add the onion and cook until softened, about 7 minutes. Add the garlic and cook for another minute.

Combine the cream cheese and mayonnaise in a medium bowl. Add the sautéed onion and garlic, Worcestershire sauce, lemon juice, Parmesan cheese, pepper jack cheese, and cayenne pepper. Season the cheese mixture with the salt to taste. Stir in the roasted mashed squash. Spoon the mixture into the 2 squash shells. Sprinkle 1 tablespoon panko over each squash and drizzle the remaining 2 teaspoons olive oil over the tops. Bake for 20 minutes or until the bread crumbs are golden brown. Serve with warm pita chips.

● *Makes about 6 servings.*

Tea Cake Biscotti

||||||||||||||||||||||||||||||||||||||||||||||||||||||||||||||||||||||||||||||||||||||||||||||||||||||||||||||||||||||||||||||||||||||

My great-grandmother Strahan was born in 1915, so she experienced the Great Depression. Comfort during these times was homemade. My twin great-aunts, Ilene and Alene, recall that when they were children, they loved sitting at a flour-covered table, indulging their creative minds by rolling sweet tea cake dough into long, thin shapes to form snakes and other animals. While they played, my great-grandmother simply rolled each ball of tea cake dough between her hands and flattened it into a round on the pan, leaving an imprint of her fingers on each cookie. She made huge batches, using a five-pound bag of flour at a time, and stored them in brown paper bags. She told me she liked dunking her cookies in coffee. This left an impression on me and inspired me to transform her cookies into biscotti. Hospitality was what my great-grandmother was known for, and tea cakes and coffee were a great introduction to it.

3 tablespoons butter, softened

1 cup pure cane sugar

3/4 cup cane syrup

2 large eggs, room temperature

1/2 teaspoon fresh lemon juice

1 1/2 teaspoons pure vanilla extract

4 1/2 cups all-purpose flour, divided

1 teaspoon baking powder

1/4 teaspoon fine sea salt

3/4 cup chopped pecans

Preheat the oven to 350 degrees F. Line a baking sheet with parchment paper.

In a medium bowl, beat the butter and sugar with a whisk until blended. Add the cane syrup, eggs, lemon juice, and vanilla. Mix until blended.

In a bowl sift 2 1/2 cups of the flour, baking powder, and salt. Add the flour mixture to the egg mixture, whisking until incorporated. Stir in the pecans.

Scrape the dough onto a floured surface. Sift 1 3/4 cups of the flour over the dough. Knead the flour into the dough, scraping it up from the surface as needed with a bench scraper, until it holds together and is moist but not tacky. Add up to 1/4 cup more flour if needed. Cut the dough into halves. Roll each half into an 11-inch log. Place each log on the prepared pan, at least 4 inches apart. Flatten the logs until they are about 1/2 inch thick.

Bake for 28 to 30 minutes, until the logs are firm to the touch, turning the baking sheet around halfway through the baking time. Remove from the oven and let cool for 5 minutes. Using a serrated knife, cut the logs diagonally into 1/2- to 1-inch-thick slices. For chewy biscotti, transfer to a wire baking rack to cool. For harder biscotti, return to a 300-degree F oven and bake for 8 to 10 minutes, turning the baking sheet around halfway through the baking time, until hard. Place the biscotti on a wire rack to cool completely. Store in an airtight container for up to 1 week.

◐ *Makes about 26 biscotti.*

Chocolate Oat Crisps with Goat Cheese and Strawberries

These easy crisps are perfect for serving at a ladies' luncheon, a baby or bridal shower, or a dinner party. Make the crisps ahead of time, and then assemble right before serving.

1 cup old-fashioned oats

1 tablespoon unsweetened cocoa powder, plus more for dusting

Pinch of fine sea salt

1/4 cup firmly packed light brown sugar

1 tablespoon chocolate-hazelnut spread

4 tablespoons extra-virgin olive oil, divided

2 tablespoons whole milk

1/3 cup mild goat cheese, softened

1 cup diced fresh strawberries

Honey for garnish

Preheat the oven to 400 degrees F. Line a baking sheet with parchment paper.

Place the oats in the bowl of a food processor and pulse until a powder forms. Add the cocoa powder, salt, and brown sugar. Process until blended. Add the hazelnut spread, 2 tablespoons of the olive oil, and milk. Process until smooth.

Transfer the dough to a flat surface lightly sprinkled with cocoa powder, and press lightly to shape the dough into a square. Using a rolling pin lightly coated with cocoa, roll the dough into a rectangle less than 1/8 inch thick. Cut the dough into 26 (1 x 3-inch) rectangles. Transfer the rectangles to the baking sheet using a metal dough scraper or metal spatula. Lightly brush the tops with the remaining 2 tablespoons olive oil. Bake for 6 to 7 minutes. Transfer to a wire rack to cool completely.

To serve, spread about 1/4 teaspoon goat cheese on each crisp and top with diced strawberries. If desired, drizzle with honey.

▶ *Makes 26 crisps.*

Note: I prefer using Nutella brand chocolate-hazelnut spread.

Pecan "Biscuit" Crackers

Homemade crackers are easy to make with my biscuit method. Their flaky texture is achieved by freezing the olive oil until it's ice cold.

1/4 cup pecan halves

2 tablespoons extra-virgin olive oil

3/4 cup all-purpose flour, plus more for dusting

3/4 teaspoon fine sea salt, divided

2 tablespoons whole milk

1 large egg, beaten

Preheat the oven to 350 degrees F.

Spread the pecan halves on a baking sheet and toast for 4 minutes. Remove the pan from the oven and let the pecans cool slightly.

Meanwhile, pour the olive oil in a freezer-safe container and freeze for 5 minutes. Do not keep in the freezer for any longer or the olive oil will harden.

Increase the oven temperature to 400 degrees F. Line a baking sheet with parchment paper.

Place the cooled pecans in a spice or coffee grinder and process until they form a powder. Do not overprocess or a paste will form.

Sift the flour into a medium bowl. Add the pecan powder and 1/2 teaspoon of the salt. Stir to combine. Make a well in the center of the flour mixture and pour in the chilled olive oil. Using one hand, carefully stir the oil into the flour until incorporated. Gradually work in the milk. Once a wet dough forms, begin using a folding technique to incorporate the remaining flour in the bowl. If the dough is sticky, add a little more flour. Form the dough into a ball.

Divide the dough into halves and place one half on a lightly floured surface. Using a floured rolling pin, roll the dough into a circle about 1/8 inch thick. Cut the dough into 10 rounds using a 2-inch fluted cookie cutter. Reshape the dough and cut out 5 more rounds. Transfer the rounds to the baking sheet using a bench scraper or metal spatula. Repeat the process with the other half of the dough.

Lightly brush the tops of the crackers with the beaten egg. Sprinkle the remaining 1/4 teaspoon salt on top and then use a toothpick to prick 4 holes in the top of each cracker.

Bake for 4 minutes, then rotate the baking sheet. Bake for an additional 2 1/2 to 3 minutes, until golden brown. Immediately transfer the crackers to a wire rack to cool completely. Serve at room temperature or store in an airtight container for 3 to 5 days.

◗ *Makes about 30 crackers.*

Southern "Fried" Pecans

||||||||||||||||||||||||||||||||||||||||||||||||||||||||||||||||||||||||||||||||||||||||||||||||||||||||||||||||||||||||||||||||||||||||||||||||

Fall in the South is filled with football games and tailgating, falling leaves and changing colors. My family and I take advantage of the cooler temperatures for late-afternoon walks, exploring the neighborhoods and woods surrounding my home. Each walk seems to bring a new discovery. The ground beneath a neighbor's small persimmon tree yields a crop of softened fruit, perfect for making a spread or butter. A tree shedding its first crop of pecans provides an ingredient for creating multiple recipes. One of the many ways I like to prepare pecans is to toss them in a seasoning blend and then roast them until crisp for a fried-like texture. Serve as a snack at your next tailgating event or party.

1 teaspoon onion powder

1 teaspoon garlic powder

3/4 teaspoon fine sea salt

1/2 teaspoon smoked paprika

1/4 teaspoon cracked black pepper

1/8 teaspoon cayenne pepper

1/8 teaspoon ground mustard

1/8 teaspoon ground thyme

1 large egg white

2 1/2 cups pecan halves

1/2 tablespoon salted butter, melted

Preheat the oven to 325 degrees F.

In a bowl stir together the onion powder, garlic powder, salt, paprika, black pepper, cayenne, ground mustard, and ground thyme.

In a medium bowl whisk the egg white until light and fluffy. Stir in the spice mixture until blended and then add the pecan halves. Mix well. Pour the butter over the pecans. Toss to coat. Transfer the pecans to a baking sheet and bake for about 8 minutes or until toasted. Let stand for 5 minutes before serving. Serve immediately.

○ *Makes 2 1/2 cups.*

Zucchini and Squash Pickles

Lunch at Daddy Bob's and Nanny Ida's farm usually consisted of sandwiches on homemade bread, vegetable soup, and delicious homemade pickles and relishes. My Nanny Ida taught me how to make her simple and delicious squash pickles. I've given them my own touch with the addition of zucchini and made them easy refrigerator pickles. Make any meal special with the addition of these homemade pickles, and be sure to share a jar with your family and friends.

2 medium zucchini, cut into 1/8-inch rounds

2 medium yellow squash, cut into 1/8-inch rounds

1 red onion, halved and cut into 1/8-inch-thick slices

3 tablespoons fine sea salt

1 cup apple cider vinegar

1 cup rice vinegar

1 1/2 cups pure cane sugar

1/2 teaspoon ground mustard

2 teaspoons celery seed

2 teaspoons mustard seed

Layer the zucchini, squash, and onion slices evenly on 2 baking sheets. Sprinkle the salt over the vegetables and let stand for 1 hour. Transfer the vegetables to a colander, rinse, and drain. Place the vegetables on a baking sheet and pat dry with paper towels. Transfer to a wide-mouth 1-quart jar or two 1-pint jars.

Pour the cider and rice vinegars into a medium saucepan and place over medium heat. Add the sugar and stir until dissolved. Stir in the ground mustard, celery seed, and mustard seed. Increase the heat to medium-high and bring the mixture to a boil. As soon as it comes to a boil, remove the pan from the heat and pour the vinegar mixture over the vegetables. Let cool at room temperature for 1 hour.

Place lids on the jars and store in the refrigerator for at least 4 days before serving. Pickles may be stored in the refrigerator for up to 2 months.

◉ *Makes 4 cups.*

Crispy Green Tomato Corncakes with Spicy Pimento Cheese

These corncakes let you enjoy the taste of fried green tomatoes without having to deal with the mess of frying. They are easy to make in large quantities using a muffin tin, making them perfect for appetizers. Top them with Spicy Pimento Cheese for a perfect contrast in flavors and textures.

4 medium firm green tomatoes
1 cup self-rising cornmeal
1/2 cup fat-free milk
1 large egg

2 tablespoons canola oil, plus more for greasing
Spicy Pimento Cheese (see recipe on page 283)

Preheat the oven to 450 degrees F.

Dice the green tomatoes and place in a bowl. In another bowl, mix together the cornmeal, milk, egg, and oil until smooth.

Pour about 1/4 teaspoon of canola oil in the cups of two 12-cup muffin pans. Place the pans in the oven for 3 minutes. Remove the pans from the oven and immediately spoon 1/2 tablespoon of the cornmeal mixture into each cup. Top the cornmeal mixture with 1 tablespoon of diced green tomatoes. Bake for 9 minutes. Remove the pans from the oven, and using a butter knife, flip the corncakes over. Return the pans to the oven and bake an additional 4 minutes or until the corncakes are browned.

Remove the pans from the oven and spoon 1 teaspoon of the Spicy Pimento Cheese on top of each corncake. Set the oven to broil, place the pans on the top rack of the oven, and broil the corncakes until the cheese begins to melt. Remove from the oven and transfer the corncakes to a serving platter. Repeat the process with the additional cornmeal batter and diced tomatoes.

❯ *Makes about 32 corncakes.*

PB&J Chicken Satays

Kids love finger foods and foods on sticks, and most grown-ups do too. The chicken-on-a-stick I have eaten at fairs and festivals in the States is a little different from the satay found in Malaysia. Like the Malaysian version, I marinate my chicken to make it tender, but instead of using the traditional lemongrass and turmeric in the marinade, I use Southern pepper jelly. Grilled and served with my Easy Pantry Peanut Sauce, the satays are sure to impress the kids—and grown-ups too.

Chicken Satays

1/4 cup red pepper jelly
1 1/2 teaspoons soy sauce
1 clove garlic, minced
1/8 teaspoon ground coriander

Pinch of ground ginger
Pinch of cayenne pepper
1 1/4 pounds chicken tenderloin, cut into
  1-inch cubes

Easy Pantry Peanut Sauce

3 tablespoons natural creamy peanut
  butter
3/4 cup canned unsweetened coconut
  milk (only the solid on top)
2 1/2 teaspoons soy sauce
2 tablespoons reduced-sodium chicken
  stock

1 clove garlic, minced
1/2 teaspoon finely grated yellow onion
1 1/2 tablespoons dark brown sugar
1 teaspoon lime juice

To make the satays, stir together the red pepper jelly, soy sauce, garlic, coriander, ginger, and cayenne in a large bowl. Place 1 tablespoon of the marinade in a small bowl and set aside. Toss the cubed chicken in the marinade in the large bowl. Cover and refrigerate for 1 to 2 hours.

Soak 7 long wooden skewers in water for 30 minutes before you're ready to cook. Skewer the chicken pieces close together.

Preheat a grill pan over medium to medium-high heat. Lightly oil the pan. Place the skewers on the grill pan and cook about 4 minutes on each side or until done. Transfer to a serving plate and lightly brush the reserved marinade over the chicken.

To make the peanut sauce, whisk together the peanut butter, coconut milk, soy sauce, chicken stock, garlic, onion, brown sugar, and lime juice in a small bowl. Serve the satays with the peanut sauce.

⊙ *Makes 4 servings and 1 1/4 cup Easy Pantry Peanut Sauce.*

Note: The satays can also be cooked on an outdoor charcoal or gas grill. Grease the grill grate and heat the grill to high. Place the skewers over direct heat and cook for 4 minutes per side.

Pulled Pork Nachos

Growing up, I attended sporting events with my dad and fell in love with the atmosphere, food, and fellowship. For me, it's all about the food. When I attended my first Ole Miss football game, I was delighted to find pulled pork nachos in the concession. This concept was new to me, and I couldn't wait to dig in. I have to tell you, though, I did receive a few cautionary looks from my friends who were concerned about my leaving the game in a barbecue sauce–covered dress. But, as you will find out, pulled pork nachos are worth it!

8 cups corn tortilla chips
2 cups pulled pork
2 cups shredded pepper jack cheese
1 cup Roasted Barbecue Sauce (see recipe on page 288)

1 cup Southern Verde Sauce (see recipe on page 285)
1 small jalapeño pepper, thinly sliced

Preheat the oven to 400 degrees F.

Place half of the chips in a 12-inch cast-iron skillet. Cover with half of the pulled pork and half of the cheese. Repeat with the remaining chips, pork, and cheese.

Bake for 7 to 10 minutes or until the cheese melts.

Spoon half of the barbecue and verde sauces over the nachos. Serve the remaining on the side. Top with a few jalapeño slices and serve the rest on the side.

◗ *Makes 6 to 8 servings.*

Note: I use leftover Collard Greens-Wrapped Pork Loin (see recipe on page 165).

Venison Egg Rolls with Sweet and Spicy Blackberry Sauce

One of my first prizewinning recipes was a Mexican egg roll. The prize? A year's supply of egg roll wrappers. Needless to say, this provided me with a lot of opportunities to experiment, and my family ate a lot of egg rolls. We always have a freezer full of venison, so this venison egg roll has become a dinnertime staple in our house. If you've never made an egg roll before, don't be intimidated. It is simply a rolled pocket for encasing all of your favorite ingredients, and it's a great way to get your kids to eat their vegetables. Shh! Just don't tell them they're in there. This egg roll combines venison sausage with finely julienned mushrooms, shredded sweet potatoes and Brussels sprouts, and broccoli slaw. The sweet and spicy blackberry sauce acts as a dip and provides an unexpected kick.

Sweet and Spicy Blackberry Sauce

2 cups Blackberry Refrigerator Preserves (see recipe on page 21)

1/4 teaspoon minced garlic

1/4 cup finely chopped red bell pepper

1/4 cup finely chopped red onion

2 teaspoons finely chopped pickled jalapeño peppers

1 1/2 teaspoons balsamic vinegar

Venison Egg Rolls

1 (6-ounce) venison sausage link

1 tablespoon reduced-sodium soy sauce, divided

1/2 teaspoon cornstarch

1/4 teaspoon pure cane sugar, divided

1/4 teaspoon cracked black pepper, divided

7 small Brussels sprouts

1 tablespoon extra-virgin olive oil, divided

2 cloves garlic, finely chopped

1/2 cup shredded sweet potato

1/2 cup broccoli slaw

4 large baby portobello mushrooms, sliced into matchsticks

1/2 teaspoon grated fresh ginger or 1/2 teaspoon ground ginger

1/2 tablespoon Chinese rice wine or dry white wine

1/2 teaspoon sesame oil

3/8 teaspoon fine sea salt

7 egg roll wrappers

1 banana, 2 inches of the peel removed from one end

Canola or vegetable oil for frying

To make the sauce, combine the preserves, garlic, bell pepper, onion, jalapeño, and balsamic vinegar in a medium saucepan. Bring to a boil over medium-high heat, then reduce the heat to medium and cook for 8 minutes. Reduce the heat to low and cook for 18 to 20 minutes. Remove the pan from the heat and allow the sauce to cool slightly

and thicken for 5 minutes. Pour the sauce in a blender jar and process until smooth. Use immediately or store in an airtight container in the refrigerator for up to 1 week

To make the egg rolls, remove the sausage casing and discard. Slice the sausage into halves lengthwise, then finely chop.

Combine ½ tablespoon of the soy sauce, the cornstarch, ⅛ teaspoon of the sugar, and ⅛ teaspoon of the black pepper in a small bowl. Place the sausage in the bowl and stir to coat. Let marinate for at least 5 minutes.

Cut off the ends of the Brussels sprouts, then cut into halves lengthwise. Place the halves cut side down on a cutting board and cut into thin slices.

Heat a wok or large sauté pan over medium-high heat. Add ½ tablespoon of the olive oil and swirl to coat the pan. Add the venison sausage and stir-fry for about 2 minutes. Push the meat to one side of the pan. Add the remaining ½ tablespoon olive oil, Brussels sprouts, garlic, shredded sweet potato, broccoli slaw, julienned mushrooms, and ginger. Stir-fry until the vegetables are slightly softened, about 1 minute. Remove the pan from the heat.

Add the wine, remaining ½ tablespoon soy sauce, remaining ⅛ teaspoon sugar, sesame oil, salt, and remaining ⅛ teaspoon black pepper. Return the pan to the heat and stir-fry for 30 seconds. Transfer the filling to a bowl.

Lay an egg roll wrapper on a clean, dry surface. Spoon ⅓ cup of the filling near the bottom of one corner. Fold the corner over the filling. Fold the left and ride sides of the wrapper toward the center (like a burrito) and roll tightly until you reach halfway up. Rub the banana over the remaining surface of the wrapper to help seal it. Continue rolling and tucking the egg roll toward the top corner. Make sure it's sealed well. Repeat the process with the remaining filling and wrappers.

Pour the canola oil into a large sauté pan to a depth of about ½ inch. Heat over medium-high heat. Place 4 of the egg rolls in the hot oil and fry, turning until golden brown on all sides, 1 to 2 minutes on each side.

Transfer the egg rolls to a paper towel–lined plate to drain, and repeat with the remaining egg rolls. Serve with blackberry sauce or soy sauce.

◉ *Makes 7 egg rolls and about 2 1/4 cups Sweet and Spicy Blackberry Sauce.*

Note: Broccoli slaw can be found in the produce section of the grocery store.

Szechuan Chicken Wings with Cilantro Yogurt Dip

Do you like it *hot*? In the South, even as we suffer in the sweltering heat and humidity, we continue to seek heat in our cooking: peppers, hot sauce, etc. In my recent travels around the globe, I have observed Tabasco hot sauce on tables as far away as South Africa and Malaysia. In Chinese cuisine, I experienced it in the eye-watering, volcanic heat of the Szechuan dishes, which use chile peppers and Szechuan peppercorns. For thousands of years, people have added spice to their foods, some to gain the benefits of the capsaicin compound found in peppers, which, research has shown, has health benefits. This Chinese version of hot wings with Szechuan peppercorns fits the bill, and the cooling yogurt dip will help put out the fire.

Wing Sauce

2 tablespoons butter

4 tablespoons hot pepper sauce (such as Tabasco sauce)

2 teaspoons soy sauce

1 clove garlic, minced

1/2 teaspoon grated fresh ginger

Pinch of fine sea salt

Cilantro Yogurt Dip

1/2 cup plain Greek yogurt

1/4 cup mayonnaise

2 cloves garlic, roughly chopped

2 tablespoons fresh cilantro leaves

Pinch of fine sea salt

Szechuan Chicken Wings

4 pounds (about 12) chicken wings

2 teaspoons Szechuan peppercorns

1/2 cup soy sauce

1/4 cup molasses

2 tablespoons minced garlic

2 tablespoons grated fresh ginger

2 teaspoons Chinese five-spice powder

To make the sauce, mix together the butter, hot pepper sauce, soy sauce, garlic, ginger, and salt in a microwave-safe bowl and microwave for 30 to 45 seconds, until the butter has melted. Whisk to blend well.

To make the dip, place the yogurt, mayonnaise, garlic, cilantro, and salt in the bowl of a food processor. Process until very smooth, about 1 minute. Spoon into a small bowl and refrigerate until ready to use.

To make the wings, trim the tips of the chicken wings and discard.

Crush the peppercorns with a mortar and pestle or rolling pin.

Combine the soy sauce, molasses, minced garlic, ginger, five-spice powder, and crushed peppercorns in a small bowl. Rub the marinade all over the chicken wings, place them in a 9 x 13-inch glass baking dish, cover, and let marinate in the refrigerator for 8 hours or overnight.

Preheat the oven to 425 degrees F. Line a rimmed baking sheet with parchment paper. Place the wings on the baking sheet and bake for 30 minutes on the middle rack of the oven.

Remove from the oven and transfer the wings to a wire rack. Place the rack on the baking sheet, return the wings to the oven, and bake for an additional 10 minutes. Lightly brush both sides of the wings with the Wing Sauce. Let wings stand for a few minutes before serving with the Cilantro Yogurt Dip.

◉ *Makes 6 servings, about 1/2 cup of Wing Sauce, and 3/4 cup of Cilantro Yogurt Dip.*

Deviled Eggs

For me, deviled eggs bring back memories of holiday dinners. My grandmother Ann Miller, lovingly known as WaWa, first prepared these for my dad at Thanksgiving and Christmas. They became a favorite appetizer of my younger sister Brittyn, who has taken on the job of making them for our family gatherings. Our time-honored recipe is simple and uses farm-fresh eggs, a really good mayonnaise, the peppery taste of tiny gratings of sweet gherkins, and a dusting of smoked paprika for flavor and "prettiness."

6 large eggs

2 small gherkin pickles

2 tablespoons plus 2 teaspoons
 mayonnaise

Pinch of fine sea salt

Pinch of cracked black pepper

1/8 teaspoon paprika

Place the eggs in a medium saucepan and cover with water. Bring to a boil over medium-high heat. Boil for 4 minutes. Remove the pan from the heat, cover with a lid, and let stand for 10 minutes. Pour out the hot water and add cold water to the pan. Peel the eggs once they're cool enough to handle, and cut them into halves lengthwise. Scoop the yolks into a small bowl. Place the white halves on an egg tray or plate. Using a fine grater, grate the gherkins into the bowl with the yolks. Add the mayonnaise, salt, and pepper. Stir until smooth and combined.

Spoon or pipe the yolk mixture into each egg half and sprinkle with the paprika. Serve immediately or store in the refrigerator until you're ready to serve.

◔ *Makes 6 servings.*

Pork "Wings" with Buttermilk–Blue Cheese Dip

We in the Southern United States, even in record-hot summers and the ever-present humidity that makes life almost unbearable at times, still love eating hot peppers and dousing everything in hot sauce. These manly hot wings are big enough to satisfy any appetite. Just make sure to serve them with the cooling Buttermilk–Blue Cheese Dip and maybe a pitcher of water.

Wing Sauce

1 tablespoon butter
2 tablespoons hot pepper sauce (such as Tabasco sauce)

1 clove garlic, minced
1 tablespoon Worcestershire sauce

Buttermilk–Blue Cheese Dip

1/4 cup plain Greek yogurt
3 tablespoons buttermilk
2 tablespoons mayonnaise
1 clove garlic, chopped

Pinch of fine sea salt
Pinch of cracked black pepper
1/4 cup crumbled Gorgonzola cheese

Pork "Wings"

3 pounds bone-in, country-style pork ribs
2 tablespoons extra-virgin olive oil
1 tablespoon Worcestershire sauce
1 tablespoon garlic powder

1 1/2 teaspoons fine sea salt
1 teaspoon onion powder
1/8 teaspoon cracked black pepper
1/8 teaspoon cayenne pepper

To make the sauce, place the butter, hot pepper sauce, garlic, and Worcestershire sauce in a microwave-safe bowl and microwave for 30 to 45 seconds, until the butter has melted. Whisk to combine.

To make the dip, place the yogurt, buttermilk, mayonnaise, garlic, salt, and pepper in the bowl of a food processor. Process until smooth, about 1 minute. Add the cheese and pulse 4 times to blend. Refrigerate until ready to use.

To make the pork, preheat the oven to 300 degrees F.

Carefully trim the fat and meat from the rib bones about 3 inches down and discard. Fold the rib meat sideways and up toward the exposed bone to create a round shape (similar to a lollipop). Secure with 2 toothpicks per rib through both sides of the pork.

Combine the olive oil, Worcestershire sauce, garlic powder, salt, onion powder, black pepper, and cayenne in a small bowl. Rub all over the pork and place the pork in a 9 x 13-inch glass baking dish. Cover with aluminum foil and bake for 3 hours. Let cool at room temperature and then refrigerate until completely cool, 1 to 2 hours.

When the pork is completely cool, preheat the oven again to 450 degrees F. Place a wire rack on a rimmed baking sheet.

Lightly pat the pork dry and arrange on the rack. Place in the oven and bake until a crust has formed on the top, about 8 minutes. Carefully remove the toothpicks and lightly brush both sides of the pork with the wing sauce. Let the wings stand for a few minutes before serving with the Buttermilk–Blue Cheese Dip.

◉ *Makes 4 servings, about 1/4 cup of wing sauce, and 3/4 cup of Buttermilk–Blue Cheese Dip.*

Coffee Milk Tea

After returning from a visit to China, I searched for a coffee shop that could make the incredibly smooth and light tea drink that had become a favorite of mine during the trip. It didn't take long to realize that I needed to re-create it myself if I wanted to experience it in the States. I worked to keep the flavor but lower the sugar by eliminating the usual condensed milk and replacing it with whole milk and my own measurement of sugar.

2 cups strong brewed coffee
6 tablespoons pure cane sugar

1 cup strong brewed green tea, chilled
1 1/2 cups whole milk

Combine the coffee and sugar in a 4-cup measuring cup. Stir until the sugar dissolves. Chill in the refrigerator for at least 1 hour. Combine the sweetened coffee, green tea, and milk in a blender jar and process until combined. Serve chilled.

▶ *Makes 4 servings.*

Coconut Milk Tea

While I was visiting China with my mom, a bubble tea shop caught our attention, and of course we had to purchase a milk tea to share. After sampling various flavors, my mom discovered her favorite was coconut milk tea. Wanting to re-create this taste for her at home, I brewed green tea and experimented until I found that the perfect ingredient to get that creamy coconut flavor was coconut milk.

2 cups strong brewed green tea   2 cups canned coconut milk
8 tablespoons pure cane sugar

Combine the green tea and cane sugar in a 4-cup measuring cup. Stir until the sugar dissolves. Chill in the refrigerator for at least 1 hour. Place the coconut milk in the refrigerator at the same time. Blend the green tea mixture with the coconut milk until combined and frothy. Serve chilled.

◉ *Makes 4 servings.*

Sparkling Lemon-Limeade

This drink, a refreshing version of our family's lemonade, is perfect for serving not only at special events, like showers and weddings, but also for lunch on a hot summer day. With a mixture of four parts lemon juice to one part lime juice, sugar, and sparkling water, it is quick and easy to make. Offer your guests colored sugar (or salt) for rimming their glasses to really make it a party.

1 cup fresh lemon juice

6 tablespoons fresh lime juice

1 1/3 cups pure cane sugar

4 cups sparkling water

Place the lemon juice, lime juice, and sugar in a glass pitcher. Stir until the sugar dissolves. Add the sparkling water and stir to combine. Serve over ice.

● *Makes 6 to 8 servings.*

Soups, Salads, and Sandwiches

My mom, my sisters, and I take every opportunity to have a little girl time together. We have enjoyed trips to Los Angeles, New York, and even as far away as South Africa. We enjoy shopping and, of course, eating. My oldest sister Leslie's favorite food is the sandwich. I still remember our trip to Philadelphia and her quest to find the best cheesesteak sandwich. On another trip, Leslie and I visited a deli and became such big fans of the Reuben that I came home and created a version just for this cookbook. While we like delicious large sandwiches, we also enjoy the small, delicate sandwiches that are served with high tea, chicken salad being our favorite. From big to small, from hearty to delicate, the sandwich, soup, and salad recipes here will become favorites of your family and friends.

White Corn Soup

Roasted Butternut Squash Soup

Mom's Goulash

Spanish Bean Soup

Individual Southern Layered Salads with Pea Pesto

Gazpacho Salad

Seasonal Arugula Salad

Acini di Pepe Pasta Salad

Creole Succotash Salad

Strawberry Salad

Dill Tuna Salad

Steamed Biscuit Buns

Cornmeal Tarts

Meatloaf Po' Boy

Mississippi Banh Mi

Mississippi Reuben

Chicken Salad Tea Sandwiches

Rosemary Honey Chicken and Biscuits

White Corn Soup

Corn was the main crop in my dad's small garden one year, and my family and I spent long hours shucking, blanching, and freezing the bumper crop that came in. The result was a lot of corn recipes. I've incorporated corn's sweet flavor in many of the dishes in this book, but if you try only one, make it this White Corn Soup. From the first creamy spoonful, you will taste the picked-at-the-peak-of-freshness taste that makes the soup elegant enough for fancy dinner guests.

Toasted Cornbread Crumbs

2 slices leftover Crunchy Skillet
    Cornbread (see recipe on page 121)

1/2 teaspoon olive oil

White Corn Soup

9 ears of white corn in the husks,
    divided

1 yellow onion, chopped, divided

1 teaspoon fine sea salt, divided

2 1/2 tablespoons butter

3 cups half-and-half

1/2 head Roasted Garlic (see recipe on
    page 290)

Chopped sun-dried tomatoes for
    garnish

Cubed avocado for garnish

Crispy bacon pieces for garnish

Crumbled goat cheese for garnish

To make the crumbs, heat a skillet over medium-high heat. Crumble the cornbread into a small bowl. Add the olive oil to the hot skillet and pour in the cornbread crumbles. Cook for about 1 minute, until slightly browned, stirring constantly. Transfer to a small serving dish to cool and slightly harden.

To make the soup, remove the husks and silk from 7 ears of corn, then roughly cut the husks into large pieces. Place the chopped husks and silk in a large pot. Reserve the corncobs. Add half of the chopped yellow onion to the pot and add enough water to barely cover the corn husks. Add 1/2 teaspoon of the salt and bring to a boil over high heat. Reduce the heat to medium-low, cover, and simmer for 30 minutes.

Strain the stock through a fine mesh strainer into a large bowl, pressing the solids to extract as much liquid as possible. Discard the husks, silk, and onion. Reserve the stock.

Preheat the oven to 400 degrees F.

Using a paring knife or corn zipper, remove the kernels from the reserved corncobs. Reserve the cobs. Melt the butter in a large pot. Add the corn kernels and remaining chopped onion. Cook over medium heat until the vegetables have softened, about 8 minutes, stirring occasionally.

Cut the reserved cobs into halves and add to the pan. Add the half-and-half and remaining 1/2 teaspoon salt. Increase the heat to medium-high and bring to a low boil. Reduce the heat to medium-low, cover, and cook for 40 minutes, stirring occasionally.

While the soup is cooking, peel back the husks from the remaining 2 ears of corn and remove the silk. Replace the husks to cover the corncobs and place the corn directly on the oven rack.

Bake for 30 minutes or until the corn has softened. Let cool. Using a paring knife or corn zipper, remove the kernels from the cob and place in a small bowl. Reserve to use as a garnish for the soup.

Remove the cobs from the soup and transfer to a wire mesh strainer over the pot. Press the cobs to extract any liquid and then discard. Press the cloves from 1/2 head Roasted Garlic into the soup.

Working in batches, transfer the soup to the jar of a blender and blend until smooth, or use an immersion blender in the pan. Pour the mixture through a wire mesh strainer placed over a large bowl, stirring and pressing the pureed corn kernels against the strainer to extract the liquid. Stir 2 1/2 cups of the corn stock into the bowl until combined. Reserve the additional stock for another recipe. Season the soup with salt to taste. Serve at room temperature, or refrigerate and serve cold, garnished with the roasted corn kernels, Toasted Cornbread Crumbs, sun-dried tomatoes, avocado, bacon, and goat cheese.

◑ *Makes 6 to 8 servings.*

Roasted Butternut Squash Soup

On one of our first trips to New York, my mom and I ate at a unique market-restaurant called Eataly. We enjoyed for the first time the light texture and deliciously creamy taste of butternut squash ravioli. Since then butternut squash has become one of my favorite ingredients in soups, sauces, and fillings. Similar to pumpkin, it has a mildly sweet and nutty flavor. In this soup recipe, I first roast the butternut squash to intensify the flavor and then puree it. Using the Eataly dish as inspiration, I added cheese tortellini pasta for added texture and then finished it off with a crumble of soft goat cheese.

1 (3-pound) butternut squash

1 1/2 tablespoons plus 1 teaspoon extra-virgin olive oil, divided

1/2 teaspoon fine sea salt, divided

1/2 cup diced yellow onion

2 cloves garlic, minced

3/4 cup low-sodium chicken broth

3/4 cup canned coconut milk

1 1/2 cups frozen cheese tortellini

1/2 tablespoon butter

2 tablespoons softened goat cheese

18 Fried Sage Leaves (see recipe on page 290)

1 1/2 tablespoons finely chopped pecans, toasted, optional

Preheat the oven to 400 degrees F. Line a baking sheet with aluminum foil.

Peel half of the butternut squash lengthwise and then cut in half lengthwise. Scoop out the seeds from both halves. Place the unpeeled half, cut side up, on one end of the pan. Cut the peeled half into 1/2-inch cubes. Place the cubes on the other end of the pan. Coat both sides of the butternut squash half with 1/2 tablespoon of the olive oil. Drizzle 1 tablespoon of the oil over the cubes and toss to coat. Sprinkle 1/4 teaspoon of the salt over the cubes.

Bake for 30 minutes, gently tossing the cubed butternut squash halfway through the baking time. Let cool for about 8 minutes. Scoop the pulp from the butternut squash half and transfer to a blender.

Place the remaining 1 teaspoon olive oil in a small sauté pan. Add the onion and cook over medium heat for 6 minutes, stirring occasionally. Stir in the garlic and cook for another 2 minutes. Spoon the sautéed onion mixture into the blender. Add the chicken broth and coconut milk and remaining 1/4 teaspoon salt to the blender and blend until smooth. Pour the mixture into a medium saucepan. Stir in the roasted butternut squash cubes and cook over low heat until warm.

Fill a medium saucepan three-quarters full with water and bring to a boil over medium-high heat. Add the tortellini and cook until al dente, about 3 minutes. Drain well.

Place a medium sauté pan over medium-high heat. Add the butter and heat until melted. Add the pasta. Cook until lightly toasted on all sides, about 1 minute.

To serve, spoon the soup into bowls and top with toasted pasta, crumbled goat cheese, Fried Sage Leaves, and toasted pecans, if using.

● *Makes 4 to 6 servings.*

Mom's Goulash

Before Hamburger Helper became popular, my mom learned how to cook one-pot family meals as part of her home economics class in high school. The meal she liked most included tomatoes, pasta, ground beef, and corn as the main ingredients. She often served this favorite meal to my family when I was growing up, usually alongside a green salad and bread. With a few slight variations in ingredients and spices, I've re-created my mom's goulash.

2 pounds ground beef

1 (10-ounce) package frozen vegetable seasoning blend, thawed and drained

4 cloves garlic, minced

1 tablespoon tomato paste

1 (28-ounce) can diced tomatoes

1 (15-ounce) can tomato sauce

1 (12-ounce) package frozen sweet corn kernels, thawed and drained

2 1/2 cups beef stock

1 tablespoon chili powder

1 1/2 teaspoons fine sea salt

3/4 teaspoon smoked paprika

1/8 teaspoon cracked black pepper

Pinch of cayenne pepper

1/2 (6-ounce) package egg white dumpling noodles

2 tablespoons chopped chives or green onions

1/4 cup cilantro leaves

1/2 cup plain Greek yogurt or sour cream

Place the ground beef in a large pot or Dutch oven and cook over medium-high heat, breaking up the meat as it cooks, until the meat is brown and no pink remains. Spoon out the excess fat. Stir in the seasoning blend, garlic, and tomato paste. Reduce the heat to medium and cook for 1 minute. Add the diced tomatoes, tomato sauce, corn, beef stock, chili powder, salt, paprika, black pepper, and cayenne. Stir until combined. Gently stir in the noodles.

Cover and cook over medium to medium-low heat until the noodles are done, about 25 minutes, gently stirring occasionally. Season the goulash with salt to taste. Serve warm, topped with the chives, cilantro, and a dollop of Greek yogurt.

◐ *Makes 8 servings.*

Note: I prefer to use No Yolks dumpling noodles.

Spanish Bean Soup

||||||||||||||||||||||||||||||||||||||||||||||||||||||||||||||||||||||||||||||||||||||||||||||||||||||||||||||||||||||||||||||||||||||||||||||||||||||||||||||||||||

My life changed dramatically in the last few months of my engagement, expanding to include a new family in Florida. Time spent visiting my now-husband's home always meant opportunities to cook for his family and learn about new ingredients and dishes. One of the dishes that my mother-in-law, Stephanie, is famous for is her Spanish bean soup with chorizo, an ingredient that's easy to find in her heavily Spanish-influenced area. In this recipe I've replaced the chorizo with andouille, similar in its spiced flavor, and replaced her Cuban bread with French bread, similar in its crusty texture. If you live in another region, you can easily swap in your local meat and bread as well.

2 tablespoons extra-virgin olive oil

1 large onion, finely chopped

2 celery ribs, finely chopped

6 cloves garlic, minced

4 red potatoes, cut into 1/2-inch cubes

3 cups cooked ham, cut into 1/2-inch cubes

1 (12-ounce) smoked andouille sausage, cut into 1/2-inch cubes

2 (15 1/2-ounce) cans chickpeas, drained and rinsed

1 teaspoon saffron threads

1/2 teaspoon smoked paprika

1/2 teaspoon smoked salt

1/8 teaspoon cracked black pepper

4 cups unsalted chicken stock

French bread

In a medium sauté pan, heat the olive oil over medium heat. Add the onion and celery and cook until the vegetables are translucent, about 8 minutes, stirring occasionally. Add the garlic and cook for 1 minute. Transfer the vegetables to a 6-quart slow cooker.

Add the red potatoes, ham, sausage, chickpeas, saffron, paprika, salt, pepper, and chicken stock and stir to combine. Cover and cook on low for 5 to 5 1/2 hours. Skim off the fat that forms on top and season the soup with additional salt if needed. Serve warm with bread.

● *Makes 4 to 6 servings.*

Note: If you do not have leftover ham, purchase and cube a 1-pound ham steak.

Individual Southern Layered Salads with Pea Pesto

One of my favorite Southern salads is the seven-layer salad. Pretty as a picture, the classic salad layers include crisp green lettuce, juicy red tomatoes, sliced boiled eggs, chopped celery, tiny green peas, flavorful bacon pieces, and bright yellow shredded cheese. You don't need to wait for that next family get-together or picnic to make this special salad. In this individually portioned salad, I've replaced the tiny green pea layer with my creamy pea pesto, placing it at the bottom of each plate or dish and then stacking the other layers on top. The creaminess of the pea pesto layer means you can eliminate the traditional rich mayonnaise topping (and the calories that go with it).

Salad

Pea Pesto (see recipe on page 280)
3/4 cup fresh corn kernels
12 grape tomatoes, cut into halves
2 cups chopped romaine lettuce

2 large hard-boiled eggs, thinly sliced
1/3 cup shredded sharp Cheddar cheese
2 cooked bacon slices, chopped

Vinaigrette

2 tablespoons rice vinegar
2 tablespoons fresh lemon juice
1/4 teaspoon sea salt

1/4 teaspoon cracked black pepper
1/2 cup extra-virgin olive oil

To make the salads, divide the Pea Pesto among 4 small glass salad bowls or mini trifle dishes. Smooth to coat the bottom of the bowls evenly. Layer the corn, tomatoes, lettuce, egg, cheese, and bacon over the pesto.

To make the vinaigrette, combine the vinegar, lemon juice, salt, and pepper in a small bowl. Whisk in the olive oil until emulsified. Serve the individual layered salads with the vinaigrette.

◗ *Makes 4 servings.*

Gazpacho Salad

||||||||||||||||||||||||||||||||||||||||||||||||||||||||||||||||||||||||||||||||||||||||||||||||||||||||||||||||||||||||||||||||||||||||||

My family celebrates the Fourth of July on the farm most years. It's a celebration not only of Independence Day but also of my mom's birthday. Fireworks, family and friends, and good food are all key ingredients of our party. The menu includes everything from barbecue to homemade ice cream to my mom's favorite, watermelon. Inspired by her love of the sweet, juicy red fruit with a sprinkling of salt, I made this Gazpacho Salad. The chilled watermelon balls, balsamic glaze, and salty feta cheese transform the usual simple slice of watermelon into an over-the-top salad.

3/4 cup balsamic vinegar

2 teaspoons pure cane sugar

5 cups watermelon balls, from about 1/2 seedless watermelon

12 cherry or grape tomatoes, cut into halves lengthwise

Pinch of flaked sea salt

2 tablespoons crumbled feta cheese

11 fresh mint leaves

In a small saucepan mix together the vinegar and sugar. Bring to a boil over medium-high heat, stirring constantly until the sugar dissolves. Reduce the heat to low and simmer until the glaze thickens to a syrupy consistency. Use a rubber spatula to scrape into a small container. Let cool completely.

Place the watermelon balls and tomatoes in a large serving bowl. Sprinkle with the salt, feta cheese, and mint leaves. Drizzle the balsamic glaze on top or serve alongside.

◗ *Makes 4 servings.*

Seasonal Arugula Salad

Salads are almost always on the menu at my house, so my Seasonal Arugula Salad is a hit! This is a wonderfully versatile recipe that can be adjusted by changing the fruits, vegetables, or greens to match what is seasonally available in your area. Tossed in a homemade citrus vinaigrette and served with homemade Buttermilk Ricotta Cheese and Cinnamon and Sugar Crisps, this isn't your average salad.

Salad

3 slices prosciutto (about 1 1/2 ounces)
1/2 teaspoon extra-virgin olive oil
10 fresh figs, cut into 1/4-inch slices
3 ounces baby arugula

Buttermilk Ricotta Cheese (see recipe on page 43)
Cracked black pepper, to taste
4 Cinnamon and Sugar Crisps for garnish (see recipe on page 46)

Citrus Vinaigrette

1 tablespoon fresh lemon juice
1 tablespoon fresh orange juice
1 teaspoon honey

1/4 cup extra-virgin olive oil
Pinch of fine sea salt

To make the salad, preheat the oven to 375 degrees F. Line a baking sheet with parchment paper.

Lay the prosciutto flat on the pan and bake until the fat turns golden brown and the meat is darker, 12 to 15 minutes. Transfer the prosciutto to paper towels to drain (it will crisp as it cools). Break into large pieces.

Heat a grill pan over medium-high heat. Brush with some of the olive oil. Working in batches, grill the fig slices until lightly charred, 30 seconds to 1 minute on each side.

To make the vinaigrette, in a small bowl mix together the lemon and orange juices with the honey. Whisk in the olive oil until emulsified and thickened. Season with salt to taste.

Place the arugula in a medium bowl. Add a few tablespoons of the vinaigrette and lightly toss to coat.

To assemble the salads, spread 2 tablespoons of the Buttermilk Ricotta Cheese in the middle of 4 salad plates. Top with the dressed arugula. Arrange the grilled figs and crispy prosciutto around the greens. Sprinkle with cracked black pepper. Lay a Cinnamon and Sugar Crisp on each salad and serve immediately.

◐ *Makes 4 servings.*

Note: If figs are not in season, substitute peaches, apples, or acorn squash slices.

Acini di Pepe Pasta Salad

I have to admit I was intrigued by the tiny pasta known as acini di pepe when it was served as part of a fruit salad at my aunt Tina's house. Once I realized it was actually pasta, something I didn't even suspect, I became fascinated with it and had to purchase a bag and make the recipe for myself. After I tried a similar pasta in a savory dish at the Purple Pig restaurant in Chicago, the creative part of my brain went into high gear, resulting in this pasta salad that celebrates the abundance of summertime vegetables such as squash and zucchini and presents them in delicate, tiny cubes perfect for a ladies' luncheon, shower, or tea.

2 cups acini di pepe pasta
1 cup finely diced (1/8-inch-thick) zucchini
1 cup finely diced (1/8-inch-thick) yellow squash
4 green onions, thinly sliced
2 tablespoons finely chopped sun-dried tomatoes

2 tablespoons chopped pimientos, drained
2 tablespoons red wine vinegar
2 tablespoons rice vinegar
8 tablespoons extra-virgin olive oil
1/2 teaspoon fine sea salt
1/2 teaspoon cracked black pepper
4 tablespoons crumbled feta cheese

Place the acini di pepe pasta in a medium saucepan and cover with water. Bring to a boil over medium-high heat. Cook until al dente, about 4 minutes. Drain and transfer to a large bowl.

Add the zucchini, yellow squash, green onions, sun-dried tomatoes, and pimientos to the bowl.

In a small bowl combine the red wine and rice vinegars. Slowly whisk in the oil until emulsified. Season with salt and pepper.

Pour the vinaigrette over the pasta and vegetables and toss to coat. Sprinkle the feta cheese on top. Let stand for 10 minutes before serving at room temperature, or refrigerate for at least 30 minutes and serve cold.

● *Makes 6 to 8 servings.*

Note: If you can't find acini di pepe pasta, substitute Israeli couscous.

> Don't let finely chopping or dicing the vegetables scare you. Cut the vegetables in half crosswise, cut lengthwise into 1/8-inch-thick slices, and then cut into sticks 1/8 inch thick. Keep the stack of sticks together, and cut across the sticks to create perfectly diced vegetables.

Creole Succotash Salad

I grew up with grandparents and great-grandparents who lived on a farm and a dad who likes to garden, so I find it amusing to see fine restaurants boasting that their greens are fresh from the farm. I guess I've taken fresh vegetables for granted, knowing that they're always freshest from my family's garden or a roadside stand. Sweet corn, okra, beans, peppers, and tomatoes—everything I need to create my Creole Succotash Salad—comes from the farm. Serve it cold or at room temperature.

Succotash

2 cups (12 ounces) fresh or frozen lima beans

2 ears of corn, kernels cut off the cobs

1/4 cup chopped green onions

18 grape tomatoes, cut into halves

1/3 cup pickled okra slices, 1/4 inch thick

1 1/2 tablespoons chopped cilantro

1/2 teaspoon diced fresh jalapeño pepper

Vinaigrette

2 tablespoons fresh lemon juice

1 teaspoon fresh lime juice

1/2 teaspoon minced garlic

4 tablespoons extra-virgin olive oil

Fine sea salt, to taste

1/8 teaspoon cracked black pepper

Crumbled feta cheese for garnish

Chopped crisply cooked bacon for garnish

Fill a medium saucepan three-quarters full with water. Bring to a boil over medium-high heat. Add the lima beans. Cook until al dente, 3 to 4 minutes, and then plunge in a bowl of ice-cold water to stop the cooking. Drain well.

Place the lima beans, corn kernels, green onions, grape tomatoes, pickled okra, cilantro, and jalapeño in a large bowl.

To make the vinaigrette, in a small bowl mix together the lemon juice, lime juice, and garlic. Whisk in the olive oil until emulsified. Stir in the salt and pepper. Pour over the vegetables and toss. Cover and place in the refrigerator to marinate for at least 30 minutes.

Serve chilled or at room temperature. Garnish with feta cheese and bacon, if using.

○ *Makes 6 servings.*

Strawberry Salad

"I'm going to take you to a pizza place, but I'm taking you there to eat a really good strawberry salad," said my friend Brian, who served as our tour guide on my first trip to Plant City, Florida. *Okay,* I thought to myself, *that's a bit unusual.* Once I had sampled it for myself, though, I understood, and the race to re-create it began. My version gets its intense strawberry flavor not only from the strawberries in the salad but also from the creamy vinaigrette. Even my dad, a ranch dressing guy, fell in love with this creamy strawberry dressing.

Vinaigrette

1 cup chopped strawberries
2 tablespoons red wine vinegar
2 tablespoons honey

Pinch of fine sea salt
4 tablespoons extra-virgin olive oil

Salad

1/2 cup pecan halves
1/8 teaspoon coarse sea salt
7 cups loosely packed kale or mustard greens, torn into small pieces

3/4 cup or more sliced strawberries
3 tablespoons crumbled feta or goat cheese

To make the vinaigrette, place the chopped strawberries, red wine vinegar, honey, and salt in a blender jar and process until smooth. With the blender running on low, slowly drizzle in the olive oil until emulsified.

Preheat the oven to 350 degrees F.

To make the salad, place the pecans on a baking sheet. Sprinkle the salt over the pecans and bake for about 5 minutes, until toasted. Let cool, then roughly chop into pieces.

Place the kale in a large bowl, drizzle some of the vinaigrette over the kale, and lightly toss until just coated.

To serve, divide the salad among 4 plates. Top each salad with the pecans, sliced strawberries, and feta or goat cheese. Serve remaining vinaigrette on the side.

▶ *Makes 4 servings.*

Dill Tuna Salad

Memories make for happiness, and food is a part of that. I was seated on a plane next to a woman from Louisiana who was flying home to visit her grown children for Mother's Day. She told me she had put in her order: a tuna sandwich with a side of potato chips. She said it was one of her favorite things and that she preferred it to a rushed lunch at a restaurant on Mother's Day. It's one of my mom's favorite sandwiches too, so for this salad I've moved beyond the simple lunch sandwich and added fresh dill. I serve it stuffed in roasted baby sweet peppers to make it the perfect finger food.

Roasted Sweet Peppers

1 pint mini sweet peppers
1/2 teaspoon extra-virgin olive oil

1/4 teaspoon fine sea salt

Tuna Salad

2 (5-ounce) cans tuna in water, drained
4 tablespoons mayonnaise
3/4 teaspoon fresh lemon juice
3/8 teaspoon finely chopped fresh dill

1/8 teaspoon cracked black pepper
Fine sea salt, to taste
3 tablespoons very finely chopped
   cucumber
2 large hard-boiled eggs, finely grated

To make the peppers, preheat the oven to 400 degrees F.

Toss the sweet peppers with the olive oil on a baking sheet until coated. Sprinkle the salt over the peppers. Bake for about 15 minutes, until the peppers are slightly blackened and tender, turning halfway through the baking time. Let cool to room temperature.

To make the salad, in a medium bowl mix together the tuna, mayonnaise, lemon juice, dill, and pepper. Add the salt to taste. Fold in the cucumber and eggs and serve or chill until ready to serve. To serve, stuffed in the peppers, make a slit in the peppers lengthwise. Carefully remove the seeds. Transfer the peppers to a serving plate and spoon some of the salad into each pepper.

◉ *Makes 4 servings.*

Steamed Biscuit Buns

I learned to love buns when I traveled to China to work with the St. Regis Hotel on Southern food promotions. The restaurants in the hotels offered a buffet of all kinds of foods: fresh fruits, fried rice, noodles, and, of course, a variety of buns with different fillings. You can buy buns at Asian markets stateside, but I wanted to create a recipe of my own. After experimenting with my Olive Oil Biscuit dough (see recipe on page 5), I found a steaming method that worked well. These buns are easy to make with staple pantry ingredients and can be made ahead and frozen. They are great for meals or appetizers.

Buns

2 cups self-rising flour

1/4 cup plus 2 tablespoons extra-virgin olive oil, divided

2/3 cup whole milk

Fillings

Pulled pork (see Collard Greens–Wrapped Pork Loin recipe on page 165)

Sliced Smoked Brisket (see Smoked Brisket recipe on page 187)

Roasted Barbecue Sauce (see recipe on page 288)

Coleslaw for garnish

Thinly sliced jalapeño pepper for garnish

Fresh cilantro leaves for garnish

Sift the flour into a medium bowl. Make a well in the center of the flour. Pour 1/4 cup of the olive oil in the well and add a few tablespoons of the milk. Using only one hand, gently stir the milk into the flour to incorporate. Once a wet dough forms, begin using a folding technique to incorporate the rest of the milk until a moist, sticky dough forms. If the dough is too wet, add 1 to 2 tablespoons more flour. Be careful not to overwork the dough.

Transfer the dough to a floured surface and use a rolling pin to roll out the dough to a 1/2-inch-thick round. Using a 2 1/2- to 2 3/4-inch round cutter, cut out 7 rounds. Reshape the dough, roll out, and cut 4 more rounds for a total of 11.

Working with one round at a time, roll out the dough to a 4 1/2-inch oval. Lightly brush olive oil on one half of the oval. Fold the other half over on top. Repeat with all the rounds.

Cut 11 (4 x 4-inch) squares out of waxed or parchment paper. Transfer the dough pockets to the parchment squares and let rest for 10 minutes.

Place a wooden or stainless steel steamer over a pot filled halfway with water. Bring the water to a boil over medium-high heat. Place half of the buns in the steamer. Make sure the pockets do not touch.

Cover with a lid and steam until the buns are puffed and cooked through, about 4 minutes. Use tongs to transfer the buns to a plate, then discard the papers. Wrap the buns in kitchen towels to keep warm. Steam the remaining buns, adding more water to the pot as needed.

Fill the steamed biscuit buns with pork or brisket and top with Roasted Barbecue Sauce, coleslaw, sliced jalapeño, and cilantro leaves. Serve warm.

❯ *Makes 11 buns.*

Note: You can let the buns cool completely, then place them in a freezer bag and freeze for later use.

Cornmeal Tarts

Cornmeal is such a great pantry staple. In this recipe it forms the basis for a beautiful baked tart patterned after a fried Mexican *sope*. The tart is filled with a spicy ground beef and black bean mixture and topped with a refreshing corn salad. The creamy cilantro sauce adds a cooling final touch.

Cilantro Cream Sauce

3 ounces cream cheese, softened

2 cloves garlic, sliced

1/3 cup diced tomatoes and green
   chilies, drained

1/3 cup plain Greek yogurt

1/4 cup fresh cilantro leaves

1 tablespoon mayonnaise

3/8 teaspoon fine sea salt

Cornmeal Tarts

Cooking spray

1 1/3 cups water

2/3 cup whole milk

1 1/3 cups fine stone-ground cornmeal

2 1/2 tablespoons butter

3/4 teaspoon fine sea salt

Corn Salad

3/4 teaspoon fresh lime juice

2 teaspoons extra-virgin olive oil

1/4 teaspoon fine sea salt

1/8 teaspoon cracked black pepper

2 ears of corn, kernels cut off the cobs

4 grape tomatoes, sliced

1 tablespoon fresh cilantro leaves

Filling

1 pound ground beef

1 cup canned black beans, drained and
   rinsed

1 teaspoon chili powder

1/2 teaspoon garlic powder

1/2 teaspoon onion powder

3/8 teaspoon fine sea salt

1/4 teaspoon ground cumin

Pinch of cayenne pepper

1/2 cup shredded pepper jack cheese

To make the sauce, combine the cream cheese, garlic, diced tomatoes and chilies, yogurt, cilantro, mayonnaise, and salt in the bowl of a food processor. Process until smooth. Season with additional salt to taste. Use immediately or store in an airtight container in the refrigerator for up to 2 days.

   To make the tarts, preheat the oven to 400 degrees F. Spray five 4 1/2-inch tart pans with removable bottoms with cooking spray.

Pour the water and milk in a small saucepan and bring to a boil over medium-high heat. Whisk in the cornmeal and reduce the heat to low. Stir in the butter and salt and cook for 3 to 4 minutes, stirring constantly. Divide the mixture among the tart pans. Press it against the sides and bottoms of the pans using the back of a spoon. If the mixture begins to harden, wet your fingertips to press the mixture into the pans. Bake the tarts for about 25 minutes, until set and slightly golden brown. Let cool for 5 minutes. Carefully remove the tarts from the pans. If the tarts stick, run a butter knife down the sides of the pans.

To make the salad, place the lime juice in a small bowl. Whisk in the olive oil, salt, and pepper. Add the corn kernels, sliced tomatoes, and cilantro. Stir to mix well.

While the tarts are cooling, make the filling. Cook the ground beef in a medium sauté pan over medium-high heat until no pink remains, using a spoon to break up the ground beef as it cooks. Spoon out the grease and discard. Add the black beans, chili powder, garlic powder, onion powder, salt, cumin, and pepper. Mix well and cook for another minute. Remove from the heat.

Place the tarts on a baking sheet. Divide the filling among the tart shells and top with the shredded cheese. Bake the tarts for 4 to 5 minutes, until the cheese is melted.

To serve, top each tart with the Corn Salad and a drizzle of the Cilantro Cream Sauce.

◐ *Makes 5 tarts and about 1 cup Cilantro Cream Sauce.*

Note: I prefer to use Rotel brand diced tomatoes and green chilies.

Meatloaf Po' Boy

With a busy schedule and a family to feed, I love planning ahead to have leftovers that can be repurposed. Slices of my Mozzarella-Stuffed Meatloaf make great po' boy sandwiches when seared and topped with extra cheese. Be sure to get good bread: crusty on the outside, light and fluffy on the inside. I am so particular about this that I have been known to fly to an event with more suitcases of bread than clothes. Serve the Meatloaf Po' Boys with a spread of tangy, sweet roasted tomato relish and get ready to see your guests' eyes light up with delight.

1/2 Mozzarella-Stuffed Meatloaf
   (see recipe on page 162)
1 teaspoon olive oil
4 slices Provolone cheese
4 (5-inch) slices French bread

2 teaspoons mayonnaise
6 tablespoons Roasted Grape Tomato
   Relish (see recipe on page 286)
Shredded lettuce
Dill pickle slices

Preheat the oven to 250 degrees F.

Cut the meatloaf into 1-inch-thick slices. Pour the olive oil into a 12-inch skillet and heat over medium to medium-high heat. When hot, add the meatloaf slices and cook until browned on the bottom, about 1 minute. Flip the slices and reduce the heat to medium. Cover and cook for 2 minutes. Place the provolone cheese on top of the meatloaf slices and cook for another minute.

Split the French bread sections into halves lengthwise and spread both sides of the bread with mayonnaise. Place the bread halves on top of each other and transfer to the oven. Bake for 3 to 4 minutes, until warm and lightly toasted.

To assemble the sandwiches, top each toasted French bread bottom with a slice of meatloaf, 1 1/2 tablespoons Roasted Grape Tomato Relish, shredded lettuce, and dill pickle slices. Place the top halves of the bread on top and serve immediately.

⏵ *Makes 4 servings.*

Note: I prefer to use New Orleans–style crusty French bread.

Mississippi Banh Mi

Growing up in the South, I have experienced hospitality almost everywhere I've gone, from Grandma's house to local stores and restaurants. However, the idea of hospitality coming to me in the form of a food truck excites me. There is something nostalgic about the idea, reminiscent of the neighborhood ice-cream trucks we chased as kids. While visiting Los Angeles, my mom and I spotted the Kogi food truck and couldn't wait to try their Vietnamese Kogi sliders. After one captivating bite, we understood why the line was so long. My Seared Beef Tips helped me create a Southern twist on this Vietnamese classic. Instead of the traditional pickled vegetables, which include carrots and daikon, I use julienned carrots and a broccoli stalk to make the most of vegetables in my area.

Pickled Vegetables

6 tablespoons rice vinegar
3 tablespoons pure cane sugar
Pinch of fine sea salt

1 cup julienned carrot
1 cup julienned broccoli stalk

Sandwiches

4 (6-inch) crusty French or po' boy bread, split
Sriracha Spread (see recipe on page 289)

4 cups Seared Beef Tips (see recipe on page 174)
1 fresh jalapeño pepper, thinly sliced
1/2 cup fresh cilantro leaves

To make the vegetables, place the vinegar and sugar in a small saucepan over medium heat. Stir until the sugar dissolves. Pour the mixture into a small, shallow airtight container. Add the salt, carrots, and broccoli and refrigerate for 30 minutes or overnight.

To make the sandwiches, preheat the broiler.

Place the bread on a baking sheet and toast for about 1 minute or until warm and crispy.

To assemble the sandwiches, spread the Sriracha Spread on both sides of the toasted bread. Divide the Seared Beef Tips evenly among the bottom bread halves. Top the beef with some of the pickled vegetables, sliced jalapeño, and cilantro. Close the sandwiches. Serve immediately.

◗ *Makes 4 servings.*

Note: If you don't want to cut the carrots into matchsticks (julienne), you can purchase them in bags in the produce department of your local grocery. For the broccoli, you can julienne a leftover broccoli stalk or use a bag of broccoli slaw.

Mississippi Reuben

On a recent trip to Reading Market in Philadelphia, my mom, sister Leslie, and I stood in line at Hershel's East Side Deli to try the shop's traditional deli-style Reuben with its toasted, grilled bread piled high with corned beef and topped with Swiss cheese, Russian dressing, and sauerkraut. After the first bite, I was gushing over how delicious it was. This Mississippi version caters to my loves, replacing the sauerkraut with vinegar-based coleslaw and adding spice with a Louisiana-style remoulade in place of the Russian dressing. If you are not already a fan of the Reuben, my version will win you over.

Corned Beef

1 (3-pound) package corned beef with spices

1/2 yellow onion, sliced

Coleslaw

2 tablespoons apple cider vinegar

1/4 teaspoon drained capers

1/8 teaspoon fine sea salt

1/8 teaspoon cracked black pepper

4 tablespoons extra-virgin olive oil

4 cups cabbage and carrot coleslaw mix

Remoulade

4 tablespoons mayonnaise

1 1/2 teaspoons ketchup

3/4 teaspoon prepared horseradish

1/4 teaspoon coarse ground mustard

1/4 teaspoon fresh lemon juice

1/4 teaspoon fresh or dried chopped chives

1/8 teaspoon garlic powder

1/8 teaspoon ground black pepper

To assemble

16 slices rye bread

8 slices Swiss cheese

About 1/4 cup mayonnaise

To make the corned beef, place the corned beef with its juices fat side up in a 6-quart slow cooker. Sprinkle the packet of spices over the beef and place the onion slices on top.

Cover and cook on high for about 4 hours, until almost fork tender. Transfer to a cutting board. Trim the top layer of fat from the beef and discard. Using a sharp carving knife, thinly slice the beef. To prevent the sliced beef from drying out, place the slices in a shallow container and spoon some of the cooking liquid over the top until ready to use.

To make the coleslaw, combine the vinegar, capers, salt, and pepper in a large bowl. Smash the capers against the bowl with a fork or the back of a spoon. Whisk in the olive oil until combined. Toss the coleslaw mix with the vinaigrette until coated. Let marinate in the refrigerator for at least 30 minutes.

To make the remoulade, combine the mayonnaise, ketchup, horseradish, mustard, lemon juice, chives, garlic powder, and pepper in a small bowl.

To assemble the sandwiches, spread the remoulade on the bread slices. Top 8 of the slices with the corned beef and a slice of Swiss cheese. Top with the other 8 slices of bread and then spread a thin layer of mayonnaise on top.

Heat a cast-iron griddle over medium to medium-high heat. Place the sandwiches on the hot griddle, mayonnaise side down. Cover and cook until the bread is toasted and golden brown, about 1 minute. Spread a thin layer of mayonnaise on the top bread, then flip the sandwich. Cover and cook until the cheese is melted and the bread is toasted, 1 minute. Repeat with the remaining sandwiches.

Add some of the coleslaw to the sandwiches and serve immediately.

◉ *Makes 8 sandwiches.*

Chicken Salad Tea Sandwiches

In all of my travels out of the United States, I have noticed one similarity—teatime. Even in Dubai, the hotel room was furnished with a real china teapot and cups for enjoying tea and coffee. My great-grandma Strahan would have liked that; she was very proud of her silver tea set. In China my mom and I had the opportunity to experience a traditional afternoon tea with scones and finger sandwiches at the St. Regis Hotel. Bringing this experience home, I combined ingredients I love into a creamy chicken salad worthy of serving at tea or just for a family lunch.

1 cooked chicken breast

1 hard-boiled egg, finely grated

2 tablespoons julienned (1 1/2 inches long) Granny Smith apple

2 teaspoons finely chopped pecan halves

1 tablespoon finely chopped sweetened dried cranberries

3 1/2 tablespoons mayonnaise

1/4 teaspoon finely grated lemon zest

1/4 teaspoon fine sea salt

1/8 teaspoon cracked black pepper

1 large Granny Smith apple

4 tablespoons water

2 teaspoons lemon juice

8 large multigrain bread slices, crusts removed

Finely shred the chicken breast and place in a medium bowl. Add the egg, julienned apple, pecans, cranberries, mayonnaise, lemon zest, salt, and pepper. Stir until well mixed.

Slice the whole apple lengthwise into paper-thin slices, then trim the slices into 2 1/4-inch squares. Combine the water and lemon juice in a small bowl. Add the apple slices and let stand until ready to use.

Preheat the broiler.

Cut the bread slices into halves lengthwise. Place on a baking sheet and broil until the tops are just golden brown. Transfer the bread slices to a serving tray and let cool slightly.

Spread about 2 tablespoons of the chicken salad over each bread slice.

Remove the apple slices from the lemon mixture and pat dry with a paper towel. Place an apple slice on top of each chicken salad sandwich.

◗ *Makes 16 tea sandwiches.*

Rosemary Honey Chicken and Biscuits

We do not fry much at my house, so when we do, it had better be worth it. This recipe is! Following my directions for frying chicken (be sure to use a thermometer to keep the oil temperature consistent) will give you what I think is perfect fried chicken—golden brown and crispy on the outside and moist and flavorful on the inside. When this delicious piece of chicken is enclosed in a fluffy biscuit and topped with a drizzle of Rosemary Honey, you may be tempted to eat the whole biscuit on your own instead of cutting it in half to share!

Rosemary Honey

1 cup honey
1 teaspoon chopped rosemary

Chicken Biscuits

2 tablespoons butter, softened
8 Olive Oil Biscuits, split (see recipe on page 5)
4 pieces Mississippi Fried Chicken (see recipe on page 208)
8 rosemary sprigs for garnish

To make the honey, combine the honey and rosemary in a small saucepan. Cook over medium-low heat for 5 minutes. Transfer to a bowl and let cool completely. Once cooled, the honey can be stored in an airtight container at room temperature for up to 1 week.

To make the Chicken Biscuits, preheat the oven to 375 degrees F.

Spread some of the softened butter over each cut side of the biscuits. Replace the tops on the biscuits and transfer to a baking sheet. Bake the biscuits for 4 to 5 minutes, until toasted.

Cut the fried chicken breasts into halves and place each half between a buttered and toasted biscuit.

If you're feeling fancy or serving a crowd, place a rosemary skewer through each chicken and biscuit sandwich to hold it together. Serve with a drizzle of Rosemary Honey.

Makes 8 servings.

Sides to Share

Hearing the stories from my granny Christine of how she grew up almost completely vegetarian, I can identify with her and my great-grandma's love of vegetables.

As we drove the long, winding gravel drive to my great-grandma McCarter's house, I was filled with anticipation. The garden beckoned us with its lightly golden cornstalks waving in the wind, bright red tomatoes peeking through the vines, and other inviting vegetables. Great-Grandma McCarter could typically be spotted working in the garden, a familiar sight with her thin flowered apron and bonnet, faded from the blistering heat of the Southern sun. I always looked forward to finding my favorite dishes on her table: a small bowl of fresh tomato and cucumber slices floating in a pool of tangy vinegar; a chilled, crispy coleslaw with tiny bits of carrot, cheese, and tart apples; tender, flavorful greens (or peas or white beans or cabbage); crispy potato bits or okra slices; and cornbread (made fresh from corn milled in a nearby town). If I was lucky, there was also a pan of homemade apple pie, made with apples from her backyard tree.

Crunchy Skillet Cornbread

Sweet Potato Cornbread

100-Year-Old Yeast Rolls

Fried Dirty Rice

Skillet Corn

Cheesy Potato "Risotto"

Sweet Corn Grits

Roasted Brussels Sprouts with Apple Butter,
Green Apple, and Candied Pecans

Smashed Potatoes

Cinnamon and Spice Sweet Potato Tots

Creamy Potato Salad

Spiced Roasted Okra

"Fried" Green Tomatoes

Spicy Pan-Fried Green Beans

Potato Gnocchi

Coconut Creamed Greens

Chopped Green Beans and Mushroom Sauté

Acorn Squash Soufflé

Pimento Mac 'n' Cheese

Crunchy Skillet Cornbread

Just as my great-grandma McCarter and granny Christine did, my mom pours oil into her ancient cast-iron skillet, handed down for generations in my family, and places it in the oven to get sizzling hot while she prepares the cornbread batter. When she pours the thick cornbread batter into the skillet, the crisp golden deliciousness begins, and memories of my great-grandma in the kitchen are revived in my mind.

7 tablespoons canola oil, divided
2 cups fine stone-ground yellow
   cornmeal
1 tablespoon baking powder

1 teaspoon fine sea salt
1 1/2 cups low-fat buttermilk
Softened butter

Preheat the oven to 450 degrees F.

Pour 3 tablespoons of the oil in a 10-inch cast-iron skillet. Place the pan in the oven for 7 minutes or until the oil is sizzling hot.

Mix together the cornmeal, baking powder, and salt in a medium bowl. Stir in the remaining 4 tablespoons oil and buttermilk. Pour the batter into the hot skillet.

Bake for 22 minutes or until golden brown. Let stand for 5 minutes and then turn out onto a serving plate. Serve immediately with butter.

▶ *Makes 8 servings.*

My granny Christine

Sweet Potato Cornbread

When the temperature drops and the trees begin shedding their leaves, I like to hold a fall potluck supper at my family's barn and invite the entire family, including aunts, uncles, and cousins. We set up a long table outside and decorate it with pinecones and wildflowers. And then the food starts hitting the table: venison roast, acorn squash soufflé, and all the other sides you would imagine at a seasonal Southern potluck. My Sweet Potato Cornbread, a favorite of the youngest partygoers, is cooked and served in a cast-iron skillet and topped with creamy butter and a drizzle of honey. It is a bread that serves like a dessert.

Cinnamon Butter

1/2 cup (1 stick) salted butter, softened

1/4 teaspoon ground cinnamon

Sweet Potato Cornbread

1 medium sweet potato
1/4 cup plus 2 tablespoons canola oil, divided
1 large egg
1/2 cup low-fat buttermilk
1 cup fat-free milk

2 cups fine stone-ground yellow cornmeal
1 tablespoon baking powder
1 teaspoon fine sea salt
1/8 teaspoon cinnamon
Pinch of cayenne pepper
Honey for garnish

To make the cinnamon butter, combine the butter and cinnamon in a small bowl. Mix well. Use immediately or refrigerate until ready to use.

To make the cornbread, preheat the oven to 400 degrees F.

Bake the sweet potato on a baking sheet for about 1 hour, until soft. Remove the skin and transfer the pulp to the bowl of a food processor. Process until smooth.

Increase the oven temperature to 450 degrees F.

Pour 2 tablespoons of the oil in a 9-inch cast-iron skillet. Place the skillet in the oven for 5 minutes or until the oil is sizzling hot.

Combine the sweet potato puree, remaining 1/4 cup oil, egg, buttermilk, and milk in a medium bowl. Whisk until combined. Add the cornmeal, baking powder, salt, cinnamon, and cayenne. Stir until well blended. Pour the batter into the hot skillet.

Bake for 22 to 25 minutes. Turn the cornbread out onto a serving plate. Serve warm with the Cinnamon Butter and honey.

◐ *Makes 6 to 8 servings.*

100-Year-Old Yeast Rolls

Nanny Ida has always been known as the bread maker. She always says that nothing tastes as wonderful as homemade bread. When we visit Daddy Bob and Nanny's house, there is usually a loaf of fresh homemade bread, whether for toast in the morning or to make a lunchtime sandwich. Nanny Ida's famous 100-Year-Old Yeast Rolls, a recipe she inherited from her mother-in-law, are made only for special occasions and holiday dinners. She recently shared her recipe, what she calls "pocketbook rolls," with me. I've made a few changes to her recipe, just as she did when the recipe was first shared with her, but the bread-making tradition now continues with me.

1 (.25-ounce) envelope active dry yeast

2 cups lukewarm water (100 to 110 degrees F)

1/2 cup pure cane sugar

3 rounded tablespoons shortening or lard, softened

1 teaspoon fine sea salt

1 large egg, slightly beaten

7 cups sifted all-purpose flour, divided

5 1/2 tablespoons salted butter, softened, divided

In a large bowl dissolve the yeast in the water. Add the sugar, shortening, salt, and egg. Add 3 cups of the sifted flour and whisk until combined. With a wooden spoon, mix in an additional 3 1/2 cups of flour. Using floured hands, form the dough into a smooth ball. Place the dough in a lightly greased bowl. Cover the bowl with a tea towel and set in a warm place to rise until doubled in size, about 2 hours. Punch the dough down.

Lightly grease 2 baking sheets.

Sprinkle a clean surface with the remaining 1/2 cup flour. Transfer the dough to the floured surface and roll out to a 15-inch x 12-inch x 1/4-inch oval. Using a floured 3-inch round cutter, cut the dough into rounds. Reshape the dough scraps and repeat the process. Lightly press each round into a 4-inch oval. Carefully spread 1/4 teaspoon of the softened butter on one half of each oval. (You'll need about 3 1/2 tablespoons butter.) Fold the unbuttered halves over to form a half moon or pocketbook shape. Place the rolls on the pans about 2 inches apart. Let rise until doubled in size, about 40 minutes.

Preheat the oven to 375 degrees F.

Bake the rolls for 14 to 15 minutes, until golden brown. Transfer to a wire rack. Melt the remaining 2 tablespoons butter and brush over the rolls. Serve warm.

● *Makes 22 to 24 rolls.*

Note: The dough can be made ahead of time and then frozen. Allow the dough to thaw, rise, and double in size before cutting out the rolls.

Fried Dirty Rice

||||||||||||||||||||||||||||||||||||||||||||||||||||||||||||||||||||||||||||||||||||||||||||||||||||||||||||||||||||||||||||||||||

Dirty Rice is a popular side dish in the South, but after traveling to Asia I decided to add a little twist to this classic. Add shrimp or chicken to create a quick entrée.

4 ounces bulk breakfast sausage

2 tablespoons finely chopped chicken livers, optional

1/2 cup finely chopped onion

1/2 cup finely chopped zucchini

1/4 cup finely chopped red bell pepper

1/4 cup finely chopped green bell pepper

2 cloves garlic, minced

3 tablespoons canola oil, divided

2 large eggs, beaten

1/2 teaspoon fine sea salt, divided

1/4 teaspoon cracked black pepper, divided

2 cups cooked white rice, cold

3/4 teaspoon soy sauce

1 teaspoon chopped fresh parsley leaves

1 teaspoon chopped fresh chives

Place the sausage and chopped chicken livers in a 10-inch nonstick skillet over medium-high heat. Break the sausage into pieces with a spoon as it cooks. Once the meat is browned and no pink remains, spoon some of the fat from the pan.

Add the onion, zucchini, red pepper, and green pepper to the pan. Reduce the heat to medium and cook for 6 minutes. Add the garlic and cook for 30 seconds. Transfer the ingredients to a medium bowl.

Return the pan to the stovetop and add 1 1/2 teaspoons of the oil, the beaten eggs, 1/8 teaspoon of the salt, and 1/8 teaspoon of the pepper. Using a spatula, stir the eggs to scramble. Cook until the eggs are set but still moist. Transfer to the bowl with the vegetables and sausage.

Return the pan to the stovetop and increase the heat to medium-high. Add the remaining 2 1/2 tablespoons oil, rice, 1/4 teaspoon salt, and remaining 1/8 teaspoon pepper. Break up any clumps of rice, stirring to coat with the oil. Spread the rice in an even layer in the pan. Cook, without stirring, until rice begins to crisp on the bottom, about 2 minutes. Stir the rice, scraping the bottom of the pan to remove rice that has stuck. Cook for another minute to crisp. Add the vegetable and egg mixture to the pan, stir well, and cook until all the ingredients are heated, about 1 minute. Stir in the soy sauce, parsley, and chives. Season to taste with the remaining 1/8 teaspoon salt. Serve immediately.

● *Makes 4 servings.*

Skillet Corn

Following in the footsteps of our ancestors, this past spring my dad, John, mounted his vintage Massey Ferguson tractor and began tilling the soil on our family farm. Afterward he planted a variety of beloved vegetables, including our favorite, sweet corn. When the light yellow of the corn tassels faded to brown, the harvest yielded a crop worthy of recipe creation. In this recipe, your cast-iron skillet is key to getting perfectly caramelized onions and garlic, transforming them from translucent to golden brown. Cream cheese and half-and-half add richness to the sweet corn kernels.

1/2 teaspoon extra-virgin olive oil
1/4 cup finely chopped yellow onion
3 cloves garlic, minced
6 ounces cream cheese, softened
3/4 cup half-and-half, divided
4 ears of corn, kernels cut off the cobs
1/2 cup whole milk
1/2 teaspoon fine sea salt
1/4 teaspoon cracked black pepper
1 (2-ounce) jar diced pimientos, drained
1 tablespoon finely chopped fresh jalapeño pepper
3 tablespoons shredded pepper jack cheese
2 tablespoons chopped green onions for garnish

Place the olive oil in a 10-inch cast-iron skillet and heat over medium heat. Stir in the onion and cook until translucent, 5 to 6 minutes. Add the garlic and cook for 2 minutes. Stir in the cream cheese and 1/2 cup of the half-and-half, stirring constantly until the cream cheese has melted.

Stir in the corn, milk, salt, and pepper. Cover and cook for 20 minutes, stirring occasionally.

Add the pimientos, jalapeño, cheese, and remaining 1/4 cup half-and-half. Stir until well blended. Cook, uncovered, for 15 minutes. Season with salt to taste and garnish with the green onions. Serve warm.

Makes 4 servings.

Cheesy Potato "Risotto"

Kids love hash brown casserole, but moms want a healthier option. This version will please them both. The risotto cooking technique creates creaminess without adding heavy cream.

Potatoes

2 tablespoons extra-virgin olive oil

3 cups frozen diced hash brown potatoes

1/4 cup finely chopped yellow onion

1 clove garlic, minced

3/8 teaspoon fine sea salt, divided

1 1/4 cups low-sodium chicken broth

1/2 cup half-and-half, room temperature

1/2 cup grated Parmesan cheese

1/8 teaspoon cracked black pepper

Topping

1 cup crispy rice cereal

1 1/2 teaspoons butter

1 1/2 teaspoons onion powder

1/8 teaspoon fine sea salt

1/2 teaspoon finely chopped fresh chives for garnish

To make the potatoes, heat a 12-inch cast-iron skillet over medium-high heat. Add the olive oil to the skillet. Add the potatoes and cook for 4 minutes, stirring occasionally. Reduce the heat to medium. Add the onion and cook for 2 minutes. Add the garlic and 1/8 teaspoon of the salt. Cook for an additional 2 minutes.

In a small saucepan over low heat, warm the chicken broth.

Stir about 1/2 cup chicken broth into the potato mixture and cook until almost all the liquid has been absorbed, about 4 minutes, stirring constantly. Add enough broth to barely cover the potatoes. Cook until almost all the liquid has been absorbed, stirring constantly. Add the remaining broth. Increase the heat to medium or medium-high and add the half-and-half. Cook until the liquid has reduced by half, about 5 minutes, stirring constantly. Stir in the cheese, remaining 1/4 teaspoon salt, and pepper. Remove the pan from the heat. If the mixture is too thick, add more half-and-half. Transfer to a serving dish.

To make the topping, place the cereal in a zip-top plastic bag, seal, and crush with a rolling pin.

Melt the butter in a small sauté pan over medium heat. Add the cereal crumbs to the butter and cook until the crumbs begin to brown, 2 to 3 minutes. Add the onion powder and salt. Stir and continue cooking until golden brown. Sprinkle over the potatoes. Garnish with chives. Serve immediately.

● *Makes 4 to 6 servings.*

Note: For a gluten-free dish, use gluten-free crispy rice cereal.

Sweet Corn Grits

To give a rich, full-bodied flavor to a dish, I sometimes use different forms of the same ingredient. For this recipe, I combined grits, which are ground corn, with fresh corn kernels. I created corn milk by simmering corn kernels in half-and-half and then pureeing. For a silky, creamy texture, strain the puree and then add the grits and cook until tender. For a rustic, hearty texture, skip the straining.

3 ears of corn, husks and silk removed	1/2 cup stone-ground grits
1 1/2 cups half-and-half	1/4 teaspoon fine sea salt
2 1/2 tablespoons butter	3/4 cup water

Using a paring knife or corn zipper, remove the corn kernels from the cobs and place in a medium bowl. Hold each cob over the bowl and use the back of the knife to scrape it to remove any excess pulp.

In a medium saucepan mix together the half-and-half and corn. Cook over medium heat for 20 minutes, stirring occasionally. Transfer the corn mixture to a blender jar and blend until smooth. Place a fine mesh strainer over the pan and strain the mixture back into the pan, pressing the mixture against the strainer to extract the liquid and trap the solids. Discard the corn. Bring to a simmer over medium-high heat. Add the butter and stir until melted. Whisk in the grits and salt until incorporated. Reduce the heat to low. Cover and cook for 15 minutes, stirring frequently with a wooden spoon.

Stir the water into the grits. Cook, uncovered, for an additional 20 minutes until the grits are creamy and tender, stirring occasionally. Season the grits to taste with additional salt. Serve immediately.

● *Makes 4 servings.*

Roasted Brussels Sprouts with Apple Butter, Green Apple, and Candied Pecans

Brussels sprouts were not a favorite vegetable of mine growing up, and the traditional cooking method of that time, boiling, did nothing to enhance the flavor of these little gems. Since then, I have learned to love Brussels sprouts due to my favorite cooking method, roasting. To create richer flavors, I roast them in the oven and serve them on top of a bed of creamy apple butter for a little sweetness and add diced apple and Candied Pecans for crunch.

Candied Pecans

2 tablespoons water

2 tablespoons pure cane sugar

1/4 cup pecan halves

Roasted Brussels Sprouts

30 fresh Brussels sprouts, cut into halves lengthwise

2 tablespoons extra-virgin olive oil

1/2 teaspoon coarse sea salt

1/4 teaspoon cracked black pepper

1/2 cup apple butter, room temperature

1/3 cup finely chopped green apple (1/4-inch pieces), about half of a small apple

To make the pecans, line a baking sheet with waxed paper. Place the water, sugar, and pecans in a small saucepan and bring to a simmer over medium-low heat, stirring until the sugar dissolves. Continue simmering until a syrup forms, about 7 minutes, stirring occasionally. Using a fork, transfer the pecans to the waxed paper and let cool completely.

To make the Brussels sprouts, preheat the oven to 400 degrees F.

On a baking sheet toss the Brussels sprouts with the olive oil, salt, and pepper. Bake for 25 to 30 minutes, until tender and brown, tossing halfway through the cooking time.

To serve, spread the apple butter on a serving plate. Top with the roasted Brussels sprouts, diced apple, and Candied Pecans.

● *Makes 4 to 6 servings.*

Smashed Potatoes

After having smashed potatoes alongside a burger at a cute restaurant in California, I knew I had to re-create these little packages of goodness. The restaurant created a flaky, crispy skin and creamy center by frying, but I set out to achieve the same result by roasting them in the oven. Serve with Homemade Ketchup or Yogurt Aioli.

28 ounces (about 19) golden baby potatoes
1 tablespoon extra-virgin olive oil
1/4 teaspoon fine sea salt
1/8 teaspoon cracked black pepper
Homemade Ketchup (see recipe on page 284)
Yogurt Aioli (see recipe on page 289)

Preheat the oven to 400 degrees F.

On a baking sheet toss the potatoes, olive oil, salt, and pepper. Bake for 40 minutes or until fork tender. Remove the pan from the oven and increase the temperature to 450 degrees F.

Flip the potatoes over and use the bottom of a glass to smash them to a 1/2-inch thickness. Return the pan to the oven and bake until the potatoes are crisp and brown, about 8 minutes.

Serve immediately with Homemade Ketchup or Yogurt Aioli.

◐ *Makes 4 servings.*

Cinnamon and Spice Sweet Potato Tots

Crispy and crunchy treats are always popular party foods. While not typically thought of as party fare, one of my favorite crunchy treats is potato tots. The crunchy exterior contrasts with the creamy interior to create a mouthwatering combination. This sweet potato version is perfect for serving not only as a side to kids and family but also as a unique appetizer for a party. There are no fillers in these tots. I use grated raw sweet potato and baked sweet potato to bind them together, and cornstarch to create that trademark crunch. Before serving, toss them in the cinnamon and sugar mixture. I bet you won't have any leftovers.

2 medium sweet potatoes
1/2 teaspoon fine sea salt
2 tablespoons cornstarch
3 cups canola oil

2 tablespoons pure cane sugar
1/2 teaspoon ground cinnamon
Pinch of cayenne pepper

Prick holes in one of the sweet potatoes with a fork. Microwave the sweet potato until soft, 3 to 4 minutes. Let cool for a few minutes. When cool enough to handle, peel off the skin. Place in a medium bowl and mash.

Peel the other sweet potato and grate using a medium or coarse grater. Add to the mashed sweet potato. Add the salt and stir until combined.

Place a few paper towels on the counter. Transfer the sweet potato mixture to the paper towels and top with more paper towels. Press to squeeze out the moisture. Repeat until almost all of the moisture has been absorbed by the paper towels.

Scoop the sweet potato mixture by the teaspoonful and roll in your hands to form a small log. Lightly roll the logs in the cornstarch and toss in your hands to remove excess cornstarch.

Heat the oil in a small saucepan over medium-high heat to 300 degrees F.

While the oil is heating, prepare the cinnamon and spice mixture. Combine the sugar, cinnamon, and cayenne in a small bowl.

Working in batches, fry the tots until golden brown, about 3 minutes. Transfer them to a paper towel-lined plate to drain and then immediately toss in the cinnamon and spice mixture.

Adjust the heat during frying to maintain the temperature. Repeat with the additional tots. Serve immediately.

● *Makes 4 servings.*

Note: For a seasonal change, try using pumpkin instead of sweet potato.

Creamy Potato Salad

||||||||||||||||||||||||||||||||||||||||||||||||||||||||||||||||||||||||||||||||||||||||||||||||||||||||||||||||||||||||||||||||||||||

My cousin Jennifer usually makes potato salad for our big Fourth of July celebration at the farm, using a recipe that has been handed down for three generations in my family. But one year, making this revered dish fell to me. While I didn't stray from the rule that the potatoes must be warm to give the salad its creaminess, I did put my own spin on it by grating the eggs for a smoother texture and adding dill. It may have been pouring rain when I arrived and placed my potato salad on the table between the corn on the cob and the baked beans, but that didn't stop my family from enjoying an evening spent together. Once the rain stopped, we finished off the night with a bang, literally, as we set off fireworks over the pond while we enjoyed our homemade ice cream.

4 large russet potatoes, peeled and cut into 1/2- to 3/4-inch cubes (2 pounds potatoes)

1 1/4 teaspoons fine sea salt, divided

2 large eggs

1 1/4 cups mayonnaise

1 tablespoon yellow mustard

1 tablespoon diced dill pickles

1 1/2 teaspoons chopped fresh dill or 1/2 teaspoon dried dill

1/4 teaspoon cracked black pepper

Place the cubed potatoes in a large pot and cover with cold water. Add 1/4 teaspoon of the salt. Bring to a boil over medium-high heat and cook until fork tender, about 10 minutes. Drain in a colander and then transfer to a large bowl. Cover with plastic wrap and let stand for 5 minutes.

Place the eggs in a small saucepan and cover with water. Bring to a boil over medium-high heat. Cook for 4 minutes. Remove the pan from the heat, cover, and let stand for 8 minutes. Run cold water over the boiled eggs and peel.

Remove the plastic wrap from the bowl of potatoes and add the mayonnaise, mustard, and remaining 1 teaspoon salt. Stir together, pressing the spoon against the potatoes to mash slightly. Using a fine grater, grate the eggs into the potatoes. Add the pickles, dill, and pepper. Stir to combine. Season the potato salad with additional salt to taste. Serve immediately or chill until ready to serve.

● *Makes 6 to 8 servings.*

Spiced Roasted Okra

Break away from boiling! Even my mom admits that this traditional cooking method for vegetables often results in loss of flavor, as well as loss of nutrients. I love to take the vegetables we've traditionally boiled, such as okra, Brussels sprouts, and asparagus, and roast them in the oven at 400 degrees for 30 minutes or less to bring out their natural sweetness. The resulting tender, tasty bites are kid- and mom-approved! My three-year-old nephew, John Michael, loves these fresh roasted okra spears with a little dipping sauce.

1 pound fresh okra (or frozen and thawed) (about 40 pods)
1/2 teaspoon garlic powder
1/2 teaspoon onion powder
1/4 teaspoon ground cumin
1/4 teaspoon fine sea salt
1/8 teaspoon smoked paprika

1/8 teaspoon cracked black pepper
Pinch of ground cinnamon
Pinch of cayenne pepper
1 tablespoon extra-virgin olive oil
Yogurt Aioli, for serving (see recipe on page 289)

Preheat the oven to 400 degrees F.

Trim off the okra stems and then transfer the okra to a baking sheet.

In a small bowl mix together the garlic powder, onion powder, cumin, salt, paprika, black pepper, cinnamon, and cayenne. Sprinkle the spice mixture over the okra and drizzle with the olive oil. Toss on the baking sheet to ensure the pods are well coated.

Bake for 20 to 25 minutes, until tender and light brown, tossing halfway through the baking time. Serve immediately with Yogurt Aioli.

◗ *Makes 4 servings.*

"Fried" Green Tomatoes

||||||||||||||||||||||||||||||||||||||||||||||||||||||||||||||||||||||||||||||||||||||||||||||||||||||||||||||||||||||||||||||||||||||||

How can fried green tomatoes be lightened up? I have tried making and baking them every way possible to create that crunchy texture you get from frying, but I've found the flavor and texture to be disappointing. Until now! I've finally created what I would say is the best non-fried green tomato you will ever eat. The trick? Coating the tomatoes in Cornbread Crumbles.

1/2 cup all-purpose flour
3/8 teaspoon fine sea salt, divided
1 large egg
1/2 cup low-fat buttermilk

1 1/2 cups Cornbread Crumbles (see recipe on page 283)
Pinch of cayenne pepper
2 medium green tomatoes, sliced 1/4 inch thick
Cooking spray

Preheat the oven to 400 degrees F. Place a wire rack on a baking sheet.

Combine the flour and 1/8 teaspoon of the salt in a shallow bowl.

Beat the egg and buttermilk together in another shallow bowl until combined.

Combine the Cornbread Crumbles, 1/8 teaspoon salt, and cayenne on a large plate or baking sheet.

Lightly coat each tomato slice in the flour mixture, then dip in the egg mixture. Dredge in the seasoned Cornbread Crumbles, pressing the crumbles on all sides of the tomato slice until coated. Transfer to the wire rack. Repeat with the additional slices. Liberally coat the tops of the slices with the cooking spray.

Bake for 20 to 25 minutes, until tender. Sprinkle the tomatoes with the remaining 1/8 teaspoon salt. Serve immediately.

▶ *Makes 4 servings.*

Spicy Pan-Fried Green Beans

||||||||||||||||||||||||||||||||||||||||||||||||||||||||||||||||||||||||||||||||||||||||||||||||||||||||||||||||||||||||||||||||||||||||||

My mom taught me how to turn green beans into an extraordinary side dish by simply pan-frying them. This recipe kicks them up a notch with crushed red pepper flakes.

3/4 teaspoon fine sea salt, divided

12 ounces whole fresh green beans, trimmed

1 1/2 tablespoons extra-virgin olive oil

1/4 cup finely chopped yellow onion

2 cloves garlic, minced

1/4 teaspoon crushed red pepper flakes

1/8 teaspoon cracked black pepper

Fill a medium saucepan three-quarters full with water. Bring to a boil over medium-high heat. Add ¼ teaspoon of the salt and the green beans. Cook for 2 minutes. Transfer to a colander and drain.

Heat a 10-inch cast-iron skillet over medium to medium-high heat. Add the olive oil and heat for 30 seconds. Add the onion and cook for 1 minute. Add the garlic, green beans, remaining ½ teaspoon salt, red pepper flakes, and black pepper. Cook for 4 minutes, stirring constantly.

◗ *Makes 4 servings.*

Potato Gnocchi

IIIIIIIIIIIIIIIIIIIIIIIIIIIIIIIIIIIIIIIIIIIIIIIIIIIIIIIIIIIIIIIIIIIIIIIIIIIIIIIIIIIIIIIIIIIIIIIIIIIIIIIIIIIIIIIIIIIIIIIIIIIIIIIIIIIIIIIIIIIIIIIIIIIIII

I was intimidated by the idea of making homemade gnocchi until my mom and I teamed up in the kitchen and made it together one day. We realized that it was really nothing more than making Southern dumplings. And just like those dumplings, gnocchi is versatile. Serve it tossed in a tomato, pesto, or cream sauce.

5 large Russet baking potatoes
1 large egg
1 large egg yolk

3/4 cup grated Parmesan cheese
1 teaspoon fine sea salt, divided
1 1/2 to 2 cups all-purpose flour, plus 1/4 cup for coating

Preheat the oven to 375 degrees F.

Place the potatoes on a baking sheet and bake for 45 minutes to 1 hour, until fork tender. Remove from the pan. Line the pan with parchment paper.

Peel the potatoes while they are still hot, and pass them through a ricer onto the lined baking sheet. Create a thin, even layer of the riced potatoes. Do not make a mound. Refrigerate until completely cooled.

Transfer the potatoes to a clean work surface. In a small bowl beat together the egg, egg yolk, and cheese. Make a well in the potatoes and pour the egg mixture into the well. Add ¼ teaspoon of the salt. Cover the potato mixture with the flour. Work the potato and flour mixture with your hands and knead until a dough is formed. It should hold together and feel slightly moist but not tacky. (If it's too tacky, add more flour.) Form the dough into a large log.

Cut 1-inch slices off the log and begin to roll into long ropes that are about ¾ inch thick.

Cut the ropes into ½-inch lengths and toss with the flour. With floured hands, gently roll the dough into a gnocchi shape (a slightly curved C shape). Place the gnocchi in a single layer on a baking sheet dusted with flour. Use or freeze the gnocchi immediately. To freeze, place the baking sheet in the freezer for about 30 minutes. Once frozen, the gnocchi can be stored in zip-top freezer bags.

To prepare the gnocchi, bring a large pot of water to a boil over high heat. Add the remaining ¾ teaspoon salt. Drop a third of the gnocchi into the salted water and cook until they float to the top and become puffy, about 1 ½ minutes. While the gnocchi are cooking, line another baking sheet with parchment paper. Remove the gnocchi from the water using a slotted spoon and place on the parchment paper–lined baking sheet. Repeat with the remaining gnocchi.

To serve, add gnocchi to your favorite sauce.

⬤ *Makes 6 to 8 servings.*

Note: Use gnocchi as a substitute for noodles or dumplings in a soup.

Coconut Creamed Greens

Greens get a bad rap because of their slightly bitter flavor, but I love them! To create a greens dish that will please even their strongest critics, I cook the greens in coconut milk. The sweet and creamy flavor of the milk masks the slightly bitter flavor of the greens and mimics creamed spinach, a dish sure to please.

2 teaspoons coconut or olive oil

12 cups packed chopped turnip greens or kale, ribs removed

2 (14-ounce) cans coconut milk

6 cloves Roasted Garlic (see recipe on page 290)

1/2 teaspoon fine sea salt

Honey, optional

1/2 cup unsweetened shaved coconut, roughly chopped

Place the oil in a large sauté pan and heat over medium heat. Add the greens and cook, stirring and tossing occasionally, until slightly wilted, 8 to 10 minutes. Add the coconut milk and Roasted Garlic. Stir until well mixed. Cover and cook for 10 minutes, stirring occasionally. Reduce the heat to medium-low, add the salt, and cook, uncovered, for an additional 30 minutes, stirring occasionally.

Transfer the greens to the bowl of a food processor. Pulse until the greens are broken down into chunky small pieces, about 30 seconds. Do not puree. Stir in the honey to cut any remaining bitterness from the greens. Pour into a shallow 8-inch casserole dish. Season the creamed greens with additional salt to taste. Sprinkle the coconut in an even layer over the greens.

Preheat the broiler. Broil the greens until the coconut is golden brown. Serve warm.

◗ *Makes 4 servings.*

Chopped Green Beans and Mushroom Sauté

Green bean casserole is a side dish that has always found its way onto my family's Thanksgiving Day table. It's probably on yours too. Why not give it a healthy and delicious makeover? This simple version uses the same basic components of the classic but replaces the cream of mushroom soup and fried onions with creamy goat cheese and almond slices. I know your family will love this dish as much as mine does.

2 teaspoons extra-virgin olive oil

1 (12-ounce) bag frozen cut green beans, thawed

5 baby bella mushrooms, cut into 1/4-inch cubes

1/2 teaspoon fine sea salt

1/8 teaspoon cracked black pepper

2 cloves garlic, minced

1 tablespoon almond slices

1 1/2 tablespoons (3/4-ounce) soft goat cheese

Heat a large sauté pan or cast-iron skillet over medium to medium-high heat. Add the olive oil, green beans, mushrooms, salt, and pepper. Stir and cook for about 5 minutes. Stir in the garlic. Cook until the green beans are almost tender but still have a little crunchy bite to them, 2 to 3 minutes. Transfer to a serving dish. Wipe the pan clean and return to the stovetop over medium heat. Place the almond slices in the pan and cook until toasted, about 4 minutes. Crumble the goat cheese over the green beans and mushrooms. Top with the toasted almond slices.

○ *Makes 4 servings.*

Acorn Squash Soufflé

|||||||||||||||||||||||||||||||||||||||||||||||||||||||||||||||||||||||||||||||||||||||||||||||||||||||||||||||||||||||||||||||||||||||||

I love developing new, creative recipes that highlight vegetables, and this acorn squash soufflé fits the bill. The squash lends a nice sweetness to this dish that will appeal even to those who don't like squash.

2 medium acorn squash
1 cup (2 sticks) butter
4 large eggs
6 tablespoons all-purpose flour

2 teaspoons baking powder
1 1/4 cups pure cane sugar
1/4 teaspoon ground cinnamon, plus
   more for garnish

Preheat the oven to 400 degrees F. Line a baking sheet with parchment paper.

Cut the acorn squash into halves. Scrape out the seeds and stringy membrane from the centers and discard. Place the halves cut side down on the parchment paper.

Bake for about 1 hour, until soft. Let stand for 10 minutes to cool slightly. Carefully scoop out the flesh while keeping the shell intact. Transfer the pulp to the bowl of a food processor. Reserve the shell. Puree the pulp until smooth. Transfer the pulp to cheesecloth and gently squeeze to remove excess juices. Return the puree to the food processor. (Pulp should measure about 4 cups total.)

In a small microwave-safe bowl, melt the butter and then let cool slightly.

Add the eggs, flour, baking powder, sugar, and cinnamon to the squash in the food processor bowl. Process until well mixed. Add the melted butter. Pulse until smooth.

Place the squash shells in glass baking dishes. (You may need to use two 9 x 13-inch pans.) Spoon the squash mixture into the shells. Sprinkle the tops with cinnamon. Bake at 400 degrees F for 15 minutes. Reduce the heat to 350 degrees F and bake for 25 to 30 minutes, until set. Serve immediately.

◉ *Makes 6 to 8 servings.*

Pimento Mac 'n' Cheese

When my older sister Leslie babysat my younger sister and me, she served us a staple meal of mac 'n' cheese and baked fish sticks. I did not like mac 'n' cheese for many years after that. I like this version, though. It's made with pasta shells, which capture the creamy cheese sauce, and crispy panko bread crumbs take it over the top.

4 cups medium pasta shells
3 tablespoons butter, divided
2 cloves garlic, minced
3 tablespoons all-purpose flour
2 1/2 cups whole milk, divided
4 ounces cream cheese, softened

2 1/4 cups shredded sharp Cheddar cheese, divided
1 teaspoon fine sea salt
1/4 teaspoon pure cane sugar
Pinch of cayenne pepper
4 tablespoons chopped pimientos
1/3 cup panko bread crumbs

Preheat the oven to 400 degrees F. Grease a 12-inch cast-iron skillet.

Fill a medium saucepan three-quarters full with water. Bring to a boil over medium-high heat and add the shells. Cook the pasta until almost al dente, 5 minutes. Drain the pasta in a colander placed over a bowl. Reserve 1/4 cup pasta cooking liquid and discard the rest. Pour the pasta shells into the skillet.

In a medium saucepan melt 2 tablespoons of the butter over medium heat. Add the garlic and flour. Cook for 1 minute. Gradually whisk in 1 cup of the milk until smooth. Add 1 more cup of the milk. Stir and cook for 3 minutes. Whisk in the cream cheese and 2 cups of the Cheddar cheese until smooth. Stir in the salt, sugar, cayenne, reserved pasta cooking liquid, pimientos, and remaining 1/2 cup milk. Cook for about 5 minutes, stirring occasionally. Remove the saucepan from the heat. Pour the cheese sauce over the pasta.

Sprinkle the remaining 1/4 cup cheese on top and then evenly cover with the bread crumbs. Cut the remaining 1 tablespoon butter into small pieces and scatter over the bread crumbs.

Bake for 20 minutes or until golden brown. If it has not reached a golden brown color, broil on high until golden brown. Let stand for 5 minutes before serving.

● *Makes 6 servings.*

Family Suppers

Sometimes people ask one of my sisters or someone in my immediate family if she or he has ever tried one of the recipes in my cookbook. A laugh is usually followed by, "Yes! These are our family meals." Family suppers at my parents' house were varied. One night it was our take on Italian pizza, and the next night it was our take on Indian butter chicken. From the time I was little, my mom had my sisters and me in the kitchen. Each of us had a job, learning to cook our part of the family supper. It's one of my favorite memories from my childhood, and when the family gets together in the kitchen now, I'm reminded why it's still my favorite time.

Southern Carnitas with Thin Corncakes

Smoked Pork Ribs

Breakfast-for-Dinner Eggs Benedict

Mozzarella-Stuffed Meatloaf

Collard Greens–Wrapped Pork Loin

Shrimp Pesto Naan Pizza

Corn and Bacon Naan Pizza

Chicken Parmesan Meatballs

Stuffed Bell Pepper Pizzas

Seared Beef Tips

Venison Sloppy Joes

Venison Meatballs

Mustard and Herb Roasted Chicken Breasts with
Artichokes, Mushrooms, and Green Tomatoes

Crawfish-Pimento Mac 'n' Cheese

Chicken à la Spice Queen

Southern Carnitas with Thin Corncakes

Pork and the South are inseparable! Back in the day, my great-grandparents all had smokehouses and raised their own hogs for sausage, chops, and even pork rinds. Salt pork and bacon were used for flavoring everything from grits to gravy. In this dish, tender, flavorful leftover slow-cooked Collard Greens–Wrapped Pork Loin is pulled and served in easy-to-make Thin Corncakes and then topped with Southern Verde Sauce and a sprinkling of Mexican crumbling cheese called cotija. If you don't want to make the Thin Corncakes, use corn tortillas instead.

Carnitas

1/2 Collard Greens–Wrapped Pork Loin (see recipe on page 165)
1 cup Southern Verde Sauce (see recipe on page 285)

1 avocado, seed removed and sliced
Cilantro leaves for garnish
Jalapeño pepper slices for garnish
Cotija cheese for garnish

Thin Corncakes

2 tablespoons canola oil, divided
1 1/2 cups fine stone-ground cornmeal
1/2 cup all-purpose flour
2 teaspoons baking powder
1/2 teaspoon baking soda

1 1/2 teaspoons fine sea salt
1 large egg
1 cup skim milk
1/4 cup low-fat buttermilk
4 tablespoons butter, melted

To make the carnitas, place the pork loin on a cutting board, and with 2 forks pull the meat apart. Transfer the meat to a skillet. Add some of the cooking liquid or chicken broth to the skillet to prevent the meat from drying out. Cook over low heat to keep warm.

To make the corncakes, grease a cast-iron griddle with 1/2 tablespoon of the canola oil. Heat the griddle over medium to medium-high heat. While the griddle is heating, combine the cornmeal, flour, baking powder, baking soda, salt, egg, milk, buttermilk, and butter in a medium bowl. Making 2 corncakes at a time, spoon 1 tablespoon of the cornmeal mixture onto the griddle. Remove the griddle from the heat. Using an offset spatula, spread the cornmeal mixture to about a 4-inch round. Return to the heat and cook the corncakes until lightly browned, about 1 minute per side. Transfer the corncakes to a serving plate. Cover with a tea towel to keep warm. Repeat the process 3 more times with the remaining batter.

Transfer the pork to a serving platter. Serve with warm corncakes or corn tortillas, Southern Verde Sauce, avocado, cilantro, jalapeño, and cotija cheese.

○ *Makes 4 servings.*

Note: If you can't find cotija cheese, you can substitute crumbled feta cheese.

Smoked Pork Ribs

When I visited QVC, a home shopping television network, to promote my first cookbook, I saw the promotion for an electric smoker while I was waiting for my on-air call. Before I knew it, I was giving out my credit card information and it was being shipped to my home. This was actually one of the best impulse buys I've ever made. My father-in-law, a master at grilling, taught me that low and slow and an incredible dry rub were the way to coax the best flavors out of ribs. Serve this recipe with my Roasted Barbecue Sauce and watch them disappear.

Rub

2 1/2 tablespoons fine sea salt
1 1/2 tablespoons chili powder
1 1/2 tablespoons garlic powder
1 tablespoon onion powder
1/2 tablespoon ground cumin

3/4 teaspoon paprika
1/4 teaspoon cracked black pepper
1/8 teaspoon cayenne pepper
Pinch of ground cinnamon

Ribs

2 (3 1/2-pound) slabs St. Louis–style
    pork spare ribs
3 tablespoons Dijon mustard
1 tablespoon Worcestershire sauce

Oak or hickory wood chips
Roasted Barbecue Sauce (see recipe on
    page 288)

To make the rub, in a small bowl mix together the salt, chili powder, garlic powder, onion powder, cumin, paprika, black pepper, cayenne, and cinnamon.

To make the ribs, check to be sure the membrane from the underside of the ribs has been removed. If not, remove it and trim any excess fat.

In a small bowl mix together the mustard and Worcestershire sauce. Rub all over the ribs.

Season both sides of the ribs with the rub mixture and massage it into the meat. Wrap the ribs in plastic wrap and refrigerate for 4 hours or overnight.

Soak the wood chips for 30 minutes. Drain. (Read the package to make sure the chips are not presoaked.)

Prepare and preheat a smoker to 225 degrees F according to manufacturer's instructions.

Place the ribs, meat side up, in the smoker. Cook for 4 hours. Baste with Roasted Barbecue Sauce and cook until the meat pulls away from the bone, about 10 minutes. Remove the ribs from the smoker and let stand for about 20 minutes before serving. Serve warm with additional barbecue sauce.

○ *Makes 4 to 6 servings.*

Breakfast-for-Dinner Eggs Benedict

Sometimes when the familiar "What's for dinner?" question comes up at my house, I decide to serve breakfast. My Breakfast-for-Dinner Eggs Benedict is a stack, which begins with my light and fluffy Olive Oil Biscuits that are topped with corned beef, a perfect sunny-side up egg, and topped with a spoonful of warm Tomato Gravy.

6 Olive Oil Biscuits (see recipe on page 5)
2 tablespoons butter, softened
18 thin slices corned beef*
3 teaspoons olive oil, divided

6 large eggs
3/8 teaspoon fine sea salt, divided
Tomato Gravy, warmed (see recipe on page 7)

Preheat the oven to 350 degrees F.

Split the biscuits into halves and spread a thin layer of butter on each cut side. Pair tops and bottoms and place them on a baking sheet. Bake until the butter is melted and the biscuits are warm, 4 to 5 minutes. Transfer the biscuits to 6 plates.

Top each biscuit bottom with a few slices of the corned beef.

Heat 1 teaspoon of the olive oil in a medium skillet over medium heat. Crack an egg into a small bowl and then gently slide it into the pan. Repeat with the remaining eggs, leaving space between the eggs or cooking the eggs in batches to avoid overcrowding. Season each egg with 1/16 teaspoon of the salt. Cover and cook until the egg white is cooked and the yolk is slightly thickened, 4 to 5 minutes. Carefully transfer each egg to a corned beef–topped biscuit. Add additional olive oil to the pan and repeat the process with the remaining eggs.

Spoon warm Tomato Gravy over the eggs and top with the remaining biscuit halves.

● *Makes 6 servings.*

*Check out the Mississippi Reuben recipe on page 113 for preparation directions.

Mozzarella-Stuffed Meatloaf

One of my first cooking disasters occurred while making a simple family dish, meatloaf. I can't remember how old I was at the time, but I wanted to surprise my mom by cooking one of her favorites. Not quite remembering how she did it, I first browned the ground beef and then tried to mix it with an egg, bread crumbs, and milk. Sure that something was not quite right, I determinedly continued, putting it into a dish and baking it. My mom took one look, quietly laughed, and began asking questions. I've long since mastered meatloaf, and this version is downright delicious! It's stuffed with fresh mozzarella cheese and spinach pesto and topped with roasted tomatoes. Once your family tries this meatloaf, they'll ask for it again and again.

2 pounds ground beef

1 large egg, beaten

1/3 cup dried bread crumbs

1/2 teaspoon dried Italian seasoning

1/4 cup fat-free milk

3/4 teaspoon fine sea salt, divided

1/4 teaspoon cracked black pepper, divided

1/2 cup Spinach Pesto (see recipe on page 279)

6 to 8 ounces fresh mozzarella cheese, sliced

2 medium ripe tomatoes, sliced 1/4 inch thick

1 tablespoon extra-virgin olive oil

Preheat the oven to 400 degrees F.

In a medium bowl gently mix together the ground beef, egg, bread crumbs, Italian seasoning, milk, 1/2 teaspoon of the salt, and 1/8 teaspoon of the pepper.

Transfer half of the mixture to a 9 x 13-inch glass baking dish and form it into a 9 x 6-inch oval. Make a shallow impression down the middle of the loaf. Spread the pesto in the center of the loaf and then layer the cheese on top. Place the remaining meatloaf mixture over the pesto and mozzarella, forming it into a loaf and completely sealing the pesto and cheese inside.

Bake the meatloaf for 40 minutes. Remove from the oven and layer the tomato slices over the meatloaf. Sprinkle the remaining 1/4 teaspoon salt and 1/8 teaspoon pepper on top. Drizzle the olive oil over the tomato slices. Bake for another 35 to 40 minutes, until a meat thermometer inserted into the middle reaches 160 degrees F. Transfer the meatloaf to a cutting board. Let stand for 8 minutes. Using a sharp knife, slice and serve warm.

> *Makes 6 to 8 servings.*

Note: A store-bought jarred pesto can be used in place of homemade.

Collard Greens–Wrapped Pork Loin

This dish makes for a great family supper with leftovers for Southern Carnitas (page 156) or Pulled Pork Nachos (page 66). Because it's cooked in the slow cooker and wrapped in collard greens, the pork loin stays moist and tender. And the greens are perfectly cooked too.

3 teaspoons fine sea salt
2 teaspoons smoked salt
1/2 teaspoon cracked black pepper
1 teaspoon smoked paprika
1 tablespoon garlic powder
Leaves from 8 sprigs fresh thyme or
   1 teaspoon dried thyme

1 (4- to 4 1/2-pound) pork loin
5 large collard green leaves, washed
   and stems removed
1 small yellow onion, sliced
1/2 cup all-natural apple juice
1 cup water

In a small bowl mix together the salt, smoked salt, pepper, paprika, garlic powder, and thyme.

Trim the fat from the pork loin. Cut the pork into halves. Rub the spice mixture over the 2 pieces of pork.

Line the bottom and sides of a 6-quart slow cooker with 4 of the collard green leaves. Place the pork on top of the leaves. Spread the onion slices on top of the pork in an even layer. Pour the apple juice and water into the bottom of the slow cooker. Top with the last collard green leaf, cover, and cook on low for 6 to 6 1/2 hours, until fork tender.

To serve, transfer the pork and collard greens to a serving platter. Slice the pork or use 2 forks to pull the meat apart. Spoon some of the cooking liquid over the pork. Pour the remaining cooking liquid in a gravy boat and serve on the side.

◗ *Makes 6 to 8 servings.*

Note: Wrapping the pork in collard green leaves helps prevent the lean meat from drying out. The collards also lend flavor to the cooking liquid, which becomes what we call a "potlikker" in the South.

Shrimp Pesto Naan Pizza

|||||||||||||||||||||||||||||||||||||||||||||||||||||||||||||||||||||||||||||||||||||||||||||||||||||||||||||||||||||||||||||||||||||||||||||

Naan is an oven-baked Indian flatbread that makes for a deliciously different ready-to-use pizza crust. I love using pesto for a change from the usual tomato-based pizza sauce, but a little goes a long way. To keep it from being overpowering, spread the pesto very thinly, and then toss the cooked shrimp in the pesto before placing it on the naan. For a deconstructed version, toss all of the components except the naan in a serving bowl. Chill until ready to serve alongside grilled or toasted naan bread.

1/2 pound medium shrimp, peeled and deveined

1/4 teaspoon fine sea salt

Pinch of cayenne pepper

1 teaspoon extra-virgin olive oil

2 naan bread slices

3 1/2 tablespoons Mustard Greens Pesto (see recipe on page 282)

6 grape tomatoes, thinly sliced

3/4 ounce Parmesan cheese

1/2 teaspoon Asian chili oil

Preheat the oven to 400 degrees F.

Toss the shrimp in a large bowl with the salt and cayenne.

Add the olive oil to a medium sauté pan and heat over medium-high heat. Add the shrimp and cook until opaque, 45 seconds to 1 minute on each side. Be careful not to overcook. Remove the pan from the heat.

Place the naan on a baking sheet and bake for 2 minutes.

Spread 1 1/2 tablespoons of the pesto over each piece of naan. Top with the grape tomato slices. Bake for 6 minutes.

Toss the remaining 1/2 tablespoon pesto with the shrimp and divide the shrimp between the pieces of naan. Shave the cheese over each pizza and drizzle 1/4 teaspoon chili oil on top of each. Bake for 1 minute. Cut into wedges and serve.

◗ *Makes 4 servings.*

Corn and Bacon Naan Pizza

Sweet corn and crispy, salty bacon pair well together in this pizza. Naan bread makes creating homemade pizza quick and easy because it's already cooked and all you need to do is rewarm it.

3 slices bacon

2 tablespoons butter

1/4 cup finely chopped yellow onion

2 ears of corn, kernels cut off the cobs

1 clove garlic, minced

1/8 teaspoon fine sea salt

1/8 teaspoon cracked black pepper

2 tablespoons half-and-half

Canola oil, for greasing

2 naan bread slices

4 slices fresh mozzarella cheese

1 teaspoon chopped fresh chives

In a medium sauté pan, cook the bacon over medium to medium-high heat until crisp. Drain on a paper towel–lined plate. Crumble coarsely. Discard the bacon grease and wipe the pan with a paper towel.

Add the butter to the pan and melt over medium heat. Add the onion and one-quarter of the corn kernels. Cook until the corn is soft, about 10 minutes. Stir in the garlic, salt, pepper, and half-and-half. Cook for 1 minute. Transfer to a food chopper or a small food processor and process until smooth. Spoon the corn puree into a bowl.

Preheat a grill to medium heat. Grease the grill grates by lightly brushing with oil.

Spread the corn puree on the naan bread slices, leaving a 1/2-inch rim around the side. Place 2 slices of mozzarella on each naan and sprinkle half of the remaining corn kernels on top of each.

Place the pizzas on the grill and cook until the cheese melts and naan is crisp, 5 to 7 minutes. Transfer to a serving plate. Sprinkle with the chives and crumbled bacon. Cut into wedges and serve.

● *Makes 4 servings.*

Chicken Parmesan Meatballs

I created this recipe to combine the two things my three-year-old nephew, John Michael, likes most: chicken nuggets and meatballs. I used ground chicken as the base for the meatballs and then gave them a roll in crispy panko bread crumbs. John Michael loves dipping these meatballs in tomato sauce, and I bet the little ones in your life will too.

Meatballs

1/2 teaspoon onion powder

1/2 teaspoon garlic powder

1/2 teaspoon dried Italian seasoning

1/8 teaspoon fine sea salt

1/8 teaspoon ground black pepper

1 large egg, beaten

1 pound ground chicken

2 tablespoons panko bread crumbs

About 4 ounces whole milk mozzarella
   cheese, cut into 1-inch cubes

Coating

1/2 cup panko bread crumbs

Pinch of onion powder

Pinch of garlic powder

Pinch of fine sea salt

Pinch of cracked black pepper

1 teaspoon grated Parmesan cheese

1/2 tablespoon olive oil

Your favorite tomato sauce, warmed

Grated Parmesan cheese for garnish

Preheat the oven to 400 degrees F.

To make the meatballs, in a medium bowl combine the onion powder, garlic powder, Italian seasoning, salt, pepper, and egg. Add the ground chicken and panko bread crumbs. Using your hands, gently mix. Scoop about 1/4 cup of the mixture into the palms of your hands. Make a hole and insert a cube of cheese. Form the mixture around the cheese to form a ball, and place on a baking sheet. Repeat with the remaining mixture and cheese.

To make the coating, combine the panko bread crumbs, onion powder, garlic powder, salt, pepper, and Parmesan cheese on a plate. Roll the meatballs in the panko mixture to coat. Press the crumbs into the meatballs if necessary.

Heat a cast-iron skillet over medium-high heat. Drizzle the olive oil into the skillet. Add the meatballs and cook, turning often, until browned, 4 to 5 minutes. Place the browned meatballs on a baking sheet and bake in the oven for about 15 minutes. Serve with warm tomato sauce and top with grated Parmesan cheese.

◐ *Makes 4 servings.*

Stuffed Bell Pepper Pizzas

An abundance of garden peppers and a quest to make a stuffed bell pepper dish that even kids would like led to the creation of this recipe. Straying from the usual rice, ground beef, and tomato sauce stuffing, I layered pizza ingredients—in this case, cooked ground sausage, diced mushrooms, and grated cheese—into peppers. For your next get-together, set up a pizza bar and let your family and friends make their own.

4 large green bell peppers
4 ounces bulk breakfast sausage
1 cup Buttermilk Ricotta Cheese
  (see recipe on page 43)
1/4 cup finely chopped eggplant
  (1/4-inch dice)
1/4 cup finely chopped zucchini
  (1/4-inch dice)

1/4 cup finely chopped baby bella
  mushrooms (1/4-inch dice)
1/4 cup sliced black olives
2 cups of your favorite tomato sauce
4 slices fresh mozzarella cheese

Preheat the oven to 350 degrees F.

Cut off the tops of the green peppers. Remove the seeds and membrane. Place the peppers in the cups of a jumbo muffin pan. Bake for 5 minutes. Remove from the oven and set aside.

Meanwhile, cook the breakfast sausage in a medium sauté pan over medium-high heat, breaking the sausage into pieces with a spoon. Cook until browned and no pink remains. Spoon the sausage onto a paper towel–lined plate to drain.

Spoon 1/4 cup of the ricotta cheese into the bottom of each pepper. Add a fourth of the cooked sausage to each pepper. Add 1 tablespoon eggplant, 1 tablespoon zucchini, 1 tablespoon mushrooms, and 1 tablespoon olives to each pepper. Pour 1/2 cup tomato sauce into each pepper.

Bake the peppers for 18 minutes. Top each pepper with a slice of mozzarella cheese and bake for an additional 7 minutes or until the cheese has melted.

◗ *Makes 4 servings.*

Note: A store-bought ricotta cheese can be substituted for the Buttermilk Ricotta Cheese.

Seared Beef Tips

Let's face it: we're all in a hurry these days, so we're often tempted to run through the nearest drive-thru after a long day of work. But it doesn't have to be that way. Just one good decision while you're grocery shopping on the weekend will save you time and money during the week. My great-grandma Strahan taught me how to buy a large cut of inexpensive meat and create several meals out of it. I put my own spin on this method by cutting the roast into cubes before cooking (but you can also ask your butcher to do it) to create different meals. Then during the week when you don't have the time to make dinner, let your slow cooker or a roasting pan do all the work. You'll end up with tender meat that will please even the pickiest of eaters.

1 (4-pound) bottom round roast
5 cloves garlic, minced
1 1/2 tablespoons fine sea salt
1 teaspoon cracked black pepper

2 cups beef stock
1 yellow onion, sliced
2 teaspoons canola oil, divided

Remove the layer of fat from the bottom side of the roast in one piece if possible. Do not discard. Cut the beef into about 3/4-inch cubes and place them in a 6-quart slow cooker.

Add the garlic, salt, and pepper. Toss to coat the beef. Add the beef stock. Place the sliced onion on top of the beef, then position the layer of fat over the onions.

Cover and cook on high for 3 hours or on low for 6 hours. Turn the heat off and let stand for 30 minutes. Discard the layer of fat. You can keep the onions if you like. Transfer the beef to a baking sheet and set aside.

Use a spoon to remove the layer of fat from the top of the liquid. Strain the cooking liquid through a fine mesh strainer over a bowl. Season the cooking liquid with salt to taste. Pour the liquid into a saucepan and keep warm over low heat.

Heat a large cast-iron skillet over medium-high heat. Add 1 teaspoon of the canola oil and swirl the pan to coat the bottom. With paper towels, pat the cubed beef dry and then add half of it to the pan. Cook until seared on all sides, tossing occasionally. Transfer to a serving dish. Add the remaining 1 teaspoon canola oil and cook the remaining beef.

Serve the seared beef tips over mashed potatoes or rice with the pan juices and cooking liquid.

● *Makes 6 to 8 servings.*

Venison Sloppy Joes

One of my favorite childhood sandwiches was the Sloppy Joe. My mom would serve them warm as part of an easy and satisfying family meal. It's still one of my favorite dinners, especially when served with a side of Cinnamon and Spice Sweet Potato Tots (page 136). I'm always looking for fun and interesting ways to use up all the venison from my dad's hunting trips. Maybe you have a hunter in your life too. If so, you'll love how this lean meat transforms a typically heavy dish into a bit lighter fare. If you don't have venison, ground chuck works well too.

1 1/4 pounds ground venison (80 percent lean)

1/2 yellow onion, finely chopped

1 large carrot, peeled and finely grated

1/4 cup finely chopped red or yellow bell pepper

5 baby bella mushrooms, finely chopped

1/2 head Roasted Garlic (see recipe on page 290)

2 1/4 cups canned tomato sauce

3 tablespoons tomato paste

2 tablespoons maple syrup

1 tablespoon Worcestershire sauce

2 teaspoons prepared mustard

2 teaspoons rice or red wine vinegar

1 teaspoon soy sauce

1 teaspoon chili powder

1/2 teaspoon fine sea salt

1/8 teaspoon ground black pepper

Pinch of ground cinnamon

Pinch of cayenne pepper

8 sandwich buns or rolls, toasted

Place the venison, onion, carrot, bell pepper, and mushrooms in a medium sauté pan and cook over medium heat until the meat is brown, stirring to crumble. Spoon out any excess fat.

Squeeze the cloves from 1/2 head Roasted Garlic into the pan. Add the tomato sauce, tomato paste, maple syrup, Worcestershire sauce, mustard, vinegar, soy sauce, chili powder, salt, pepper, cinnamon, and cayenne. Stir well. Cover, reduce heat to medium-low, and cook for 15 to 20 minutes. Spoon onto the buns and serve warm.

◉ *Makes 6 to 8 servings.*

Venison Meatballs

Shortly after Scooter's Cafe opened in Poplarville, Mississippi, my family and I became fans of the restaurant's meatball po' boys. After sharing with Chemin, the owner, that I wanted to learn how to make her meatballs, she kindly allowed me to observe. Like most seasoned cooks, she knew her recipe by heart and added the spices without measuring. After observing her process, I made my own meatball recipe and then added an additional ingredient: Parmesan cheese. What makes Chemin's meatballs unusual is that she doesn't use bread crumbs as a binder. She said that crumbs are used to make the meat go further, and if you don't have to use them, don't! I used the tips and techniques I learned from Chemin to make these venison meatballs; you'll notice that there are no bread crumbs in these bundles of goodness. If you don't have venison, ground chuck works well too.

2 pounds ground venison (80 percent lean)
1 1/4 teaspoons fine sea salt
3/4 teaspoon onion powder
1/2 teaspoon garlic powder
1/2 teaspoon dried parsley
1/2 teaspoon dried Italian seasoning
1/4 teaspoon cracked black pepper
1/4 teaspoon cayenne pepper
2 cloves garlic, minced
1 tablespoon Worcestershire sauce
3 tablespoons whole milk
4 teaspoons grated Parmesan cheese
1 1/2 teaspoons extra-virgin olive oil

Preheat the oven to 375 degrees F.

Place the meat in a medium bowl. Add the salt, onion powder, garlic powder, parsley, Italian seasoning, black pepper, cayenne, garlic, Worcestershire sauce, milk, and Parmesan cheese to the bowl. Gently work the ingredients into the ground venison. Do not overwork the meat.

Form the meatballs by scooping 1/3 cup of the mixture into your hand and rolling it into a ball. Pour the oil into a 12-inch cast-iron skillet and place the meatballs close together.

Bake the meatballs for about 25 minutes, until done. Transfer the meatballs to a paper towel–lined plate to drain. Serve warm.

⏺ *Makes about 12 meatballs, or 4 servings.*

Serving Tip: Serve with marinara sauce and spaghetti, with a mushroom cream sauce and egg noodles, or on mini buns with your favorite sandwich toppings.

Mustard and Herb Roasted Chicken Breasts with Artichokes, Mushrooms, and Green Tomatoes

A lot of people have asked me for good chicken dishes over the years, so I created this easy one-pot dish that bakes in the oven. The artichokes, mushrooms, and fresh herbs make this dish feel indulgent. If you don't have a fresh herb garden, you'll want to buy herbs from the grocery store. The dish just won't be the same with dried herbs. Lots of love went into creating this dish. I hope you enjoy it!

1/2 yellow onion, thinly sliced

1 (14-ounce) can artichoke hearts, drained, or 1 (9-ounce) package frozen artichokes, thawed

6 baby bella mushrooms, roughly chopped

1 small green tomato, finely chopped

1/2 cup dry white wine

1/4 cup chicken stock

3/4 teaspoon fine sea salt, divided

1/4 teaspoon cracked black pepper, divided

1 tablespoon stone-ground mustard

1 teaspoon honey

1/2 teaspoon whole mustard seeds

1 tablespoon fresh lemon juice

1/4 teaspoon fresh thyme

6 sage leaves, chopped

4 cloves garlic, minced

3 boneless, skinless chicken breasts (about 1 1/2 pounds)

1/2 tablespoon extra-virgin olive oil

Preheat the oven to 400 degrees F.

In a large, deep casserole dish or cast-iron skillet, place the onion slices, artichokes, mushrooms, and green tomatoes. Pour the white wine and stock over the vegetables. Add 1/4 teaspoon of the salt and 1/8 teaspoon of the pepper.

In a small bowl mix together the mustard, honey, mustard seeds, lemon juice, thyme, sage, garlic, remaining 1/2 teaspoon salt, and remaining 1/8 teaspoon pepper. Rub the mixture on the chicken breasts. Place the chicken breasts on top of the vegetables in the pan. Drizzle the olive oil over the chicken.

Bake the chicken and vegetables for 40 minutes or until the chicken is done. Transfer the chicken breasts and vegetables to a serving platter. Pour the pan drippings into a medium sauté pan and skim the fat off the top. Cook over medium-high heat until the liquid has reduced by half. Serve the roasted chicken breasts and vegetables with the pan juices.

● *Makes 3 to 4 servings.*

Crawfish-Pimento Mac 'n' Cheese

I had lobster mac 'n' cheese on a family vacation to Boston and fell in love. Lobster isn't a local ingredient on the Gulf Coast where I live, but its cousin, the humble but extremely tasty crawfish, is. And since this is the South, I've spiced up my pimento cheese and added Rotel tomatoes. The gnocchi pasta are about the same size as the crawfish tails, and they capture the sauce to make each bite perfect. This comfort food might become your family's favorite.

3 cups gnocchi pasta shells

3 tablespoons butter, divided

2 cloves garlic, minced

3 tablespoons all-purpose flour

2 cups whole milk

1 1/2 cups Spicy Pimento Cheese (see recipe on page 283)

1 (10-ounce) can diced tomatoes and green chilies, drained

1 (12-ounce) package frozen crawfish tails, thawed and drained

3/4 teaspoon fine sea salt

1/3 cup panko bread crumbs

Preheat the oven to 400 degrees F. Grease a 12-inch cast-iron skillet.

Fill a medium saucepan three-quarters full with water. Bring to a boil over medium-high heat. Add the gnocchi pasta and cook until al dente, about 5 minutes. Drain the pasta and place it in the greased skillet.

Melt 2 tablespoons of the butter in a large sauté pan over medium heat. Add the garlic and flour. Stir and cook for 1 minute. Gradually whisk in 1 cup of the milk until smooth, then add the remaining 1 cup milk. Whisk in the Spicy Pimento Cheese until melted and smooth. Cook the cheese sauce until the mixture begins to thicken, 4 to 5 minutes. Stir in the canned tomatoes and green chilies, crawfish, and salt. Add additional salt to taste.

Gently stir the sauce into the pasta until combined. Sprinkle the bread crumbs evenly over the top. Cut the remaining 1 tablespoon butter into cubes and scatter over the bread crumbs.

Bake for about 20 minutes, until brown. If the top has not browned during baking, change the oven setting to broil and broil until golden brown. Let stand for 5 minutes before serving.

◉ *Makes 6 servings.*

Chicken à la Spice Queen

I was introduced to Indian cuisine while I was on the television show *MasterChef*, and since then I have learned to love it. This recipe is my Southern take on traditional butter chicken. The tender chicken is marinated in yogurt and served in a tomato cream sauce over rice. Instead of traditional Indian spices, I've used spices from my Southern pantry.

1 cup plain Greek yogurt
1 teaspoon fresh lemon juice
2 teaspoons minced garlic, divided
1 1/2 teaspoons onion powder
1 teaspoon smoked salt
1 teaspoon fine sea salt
2 1/2 teaspoons smoked paprika
1/2 teaspoon ground coriander
1/4 teaspoon ground thyme
1/4 teaspoon cracked black pepper
1/4 teaspoon cayenne pepper

1/8 teaspoon ground cinnamon
3 to 4 boneless, skinless chicken
    breasts, cut into 1-inch cubes
    (1 1/2 to 2 pounds total)
2 tablespoons extra-virgin olive oil
1/2 cup diced yellow onion
1 (14 1/2-ounce) can diced tomatoes,
    drained
1/2 cup plus 1 tablespoon heavy cream,
    divided
1 tablespoon cornstarch
1 1/2 cups cooked white rice

Combine the yogurt, lemon juice, 1 teaspoon of the garlic, onion powder, smoked salt, sea salt, paprika, coriander, thyme, black pepper, cayenne, and cinnamon in a gallon-size zip-top plastic bag. Stir until mixed well. Add the chicken to the bag. Remove as much air as possible and seal the bag. Toss to coat the chicken.

Heat a 12-inch cast-iron or nonstick skillet over medium heat. Add the olive oil and onion. Cook for 6 minutes. Add the remaining 1 teaspoon garlic and cook for 1 minute. Add the tomatoes, 1/2 cup of the heavy cream and chicken and spice marinade. Stir to combine. Cover, reduce the heat to medium-low, and cook for 20 minutes, stirring occasionally. Uncover, increase the heat to medium, and cook for about 8 minutes, stirring occasionally.

Combine the remaining 1 tablespoon heavy cream with the cornstarch in a small bowl. Add the slurry to the chicken mixture. Increase the heat to medium-high and cook for 2 minutes to thicken, stirring constantly. Season with salt to taste. Serve over the cooked rice.

◉ *Makes 5 servings.*

Sunday Dinners

Shortly after church services each Sunday, I fall into the comfortable routine of helping to get things ready for dinner. My cousin Andrea usually perches on a stool near the long wooden dining table at my aunt Ilene's house to chop components for a salad while I whip up a creamy homemade ranch dressing. The companionable work in this kitchen puts to rest that old saying "too many cooks in the kitchen." In this case, many hands make short work of the meal preparation. In no time at all, family members line up to fill their plates from the huge pots of rice, beans, and greens set out on the stove, and my uncle Bill says grace. It's important to my family that we always take the time to be grateful for our blessings. If your family doesn't already have a Sunday dinner tradition, let these recipes be inspiration to start a tradition of your own.

Spice-Rubbed Venison Roast

Smoked Brisket

Butter Bean Cassoulet with Roasted Grape Tomato Relish

Turkey Potpie

Chicken Enchilada Stack

Smoked Red Beans and Rice

Roasted-Braised Chicken

Shrimp and Andouille Gumbo

Spice-Rubbed Venison Roast

When hunting season arrives, my dad puts on his camo gear, gathers his hunting supplies, and sets off for North Mississippi to bring home some prized venison. A low-fat, high-protein red meat, venison can't be bought in the grocery store. For our first family supper last fall, we cooked a lean and tender venison roast. It's one of the first venison recipes I learned to cook from my mom. This version highlights the juicy tenderness of the meat with complementary spices. If you aren't a hunter, I hope you have a generous friend who is.

2 tablespoons fine sea salt
1/2 tablespoon chopped dried sage
1 teaspoon chopped dried tarragon
1 teaspoon chopped dried thyme
1 teaspoon ground cloves
1 1/2 teaspoons Worcestershire powder

1/4 teaspoon cracked black pepper
1 teaspoon minced garlic
1 (5-pound) venison roast
1 yellow onion, sliced
1 cup water

Preheat the oven to 400 degrees F.

In a small bowl mix together the salt, sage, tarragon, thyme, cloves, Worcestershire powder, black pepper, and garlic.

Place the venison roast in a 9 x 13-inch glass baking dish. Massage the spice mixture all over the venison. Turn the venison fat side up. Place onion slices on top. Pour the water in the bottom of the baking dish. Cover with aluminum foil. Bake for 30 minutes, then reduce the oven temperature to 250 degrees F and bake for 4 1/2 hours. Remove the venison from the oven and let stand for 10 minutes. Thinly slice or pull the meat apart with 2 forks. Serve warm with the pan juices.

● *Makes 8 servings.*

Note: Worcestershire powder can be found online and at specialty kitchen and spice stores.

Smoked Brisket

I've never been a fan of brisket because it's a little too fatty for my taste—until now, that is. My husband, Ryan, smoked a brisket for me that was so tender, it melted in my mouth. After I told him how delicious it was, he shared his secret rub ingredient with me: coffee. Make this recipe for family or friends who say they aren't fans of brisket, and I bet they'll change their minds too.

3 3/4 tablespoons firmly packed light brown sugar
1 3/4 tablespoons finely ground medium-roast coffee
1 3/4 tablespoons smoked paprika
1 3/4 tablespoons garlic powder
3/4 tablespoon onion powder
3/4 tablespoon chili powder

2 1/4 tablespoons fine sea salt
1/2 teaspoon cracked black pepper
1/4 teaspoon cayenne pepper
1 (6-pound) brisket, fat trimmed to 1/4 inch thick
Oak, hickory, or mesquite wood chips
Roasted Barbecue Sauce (see recipe on page 288), optional

In a small bowl mix together the brown sugar, coffee, paprika, garlic powder, onion powder, chili powder, salt, black pepper, and cayenne.

Pat the brisket dry with paper towels. Rub the spice mixture all over the brisket and then wrap it tightly in plastic wrap. Refrigerate overnight.

Remove the brisket from the refrigerator 1 hour prior to smoking to allow the meat to come to room temperature. Soak the wood chips during that hour, then drain. (Read the package to make sure the chips are not presoaked.) Prepare a smoker with the wood chips according to the manufacturer's instructions, and heat to 225 degrees F.

Place the brisket fat side up in the smoker and cook for about 6 hours (1 hour per pound), until an instant-read thermometer reaches a minimum internal temperature of 185 degrees F and maximum of 200 degrees F. Remove the meat from the smoker and let stand for 30 minutes.

To serve, trim the harder, darker pieces (burned ends) off the edges of the brisket and chop them into small pieces. Thinly slice the brisket against the grain and place it on a serving platter with a container of barbecue sauce alongside.

◗ *Makes 10 to 12 servings.*

Butter Bean Cassoulet with Roasted Grape Tomato Relish

Movie Star restaurant in Hattiesburg, Mississippi, is my family's go-to place for Southern food away from home. I look forward to the greens and the creamy butter beans on the buffet. A side of cornbread is all I need to make it a meal. At home, I prepare butter beans as a one-pot meal with pork tenderloin, garlic, and onion. I serve my tangy Roasted Grape Tomato Relish alongside for the perfect flavor contrast. Your family is going to ask for this dish once they try it.

3 slices bacon
2 pork tenderloins (1 1/2 pounds total)
2 teaspoons fine sea salt, divided
1 1/2 tablespoons extra-virgin olive oil
1 cup finely chopped yellow onion
   (about 1 medium onion)
6 cloves garlic, minced
1 (1-pound) bag dried large white lima
   beans (butter beans)

5 cups unsalted chicken stock
2 teaspoons smoked salt
1/2 teaspoon ground cumin
1/4 teaspoon cracked black pepper
4 sprigs fresh thyme
Roasted Grape Tomato Relish (see
   recipe on page 286)

Place the bacon in a medium sauté pan and cook until crispy. Transfer the bacon to a paper towel–lined plate to drain, and reserve the bacon for another use. Do not discard the grease from the pan.

Cut each tenderloin into 4 equal pieces. Pat the pieces dry with paper towels. Fold the uneven end pieces under and secure with a toothpick to form a square. Sprinkle 1 teaspoon of the sea salt over the pork. Return the pan with the bacon grease back to the stovetop over medium-high heat. Add the pork to the pan and sear on all sides. Transfer the seared pork to a plate. Wipe the pan clean and return to the stovetop over medium heat. Add the olive oil and onion to the pan and cook until the onion is translucent, 6 to 8 minutes. Add the garlic and cook for 30 seconds. Transfer the mixture to a 6-quart slow cooker.

Add the lima beans, chicken stock, smoked salt, remaining 1 teaspoon sea salt, cumin, black pepper, and thyme. Stir until combined. Place the pork in the slow cooker. Cover and cook on low for 6 hours. Remove the pork from the slow cooker and gently remove the toothpicks from the pork. Season the lima beans with salt to taste. Serve warm with the Roasted Grape Tomato Relish.

○ *Makes 6 to 8 servings.*

Turkey Potpie

||||||||||||||||||||||||||||||||||||||||||||||||||||||||||||||||||||||||||||||||||||||||||||||||||||||||||||||||||||||||||||||||||||||||||||||||||||||||||||||||||

This potpie is a great way to use leftover turkey from your Thanksgiving or Christmas meal. The crispy olive oil piecrust adds a contrast of texture to the creamy pie filling.

3 cups (1/2-inch) cubed red potatoes

Fine sea salt, to taste

3 tablespoons butter

2 tablespoons extra-virgin olive oil

1/2 cup very finely chopped celery

1/3 cup very finely chopped leek (white part only) or yellow onion

2 cloves garlic, minced

1/2 cup all-purpose flour

3 1/2 cups unsalted turkey or chicken stock

2 cups plus 1 tablespoon half-and-half, divided

3 sprigs fresh thyme

4 fresh sage leaves, chopped

1 bunch mustard greens

1/2 cup shredded Parmesan cheese

1/4 teaspoon cracked black pepper

1 (10- to 12-ounce) bag frozen green peas, thawed

1 cooked turkey breast, shredded or coarsely chopped

1 cooked turkey drumstick, shredded or coarsely chopped

2 recipes Olive Oil Pie Dough (see recipe on page 291)

Preheat the oven to 400 degrees F.

Place the potatoes and a pinch of salt in a large pot and cover the potatoes with cold water. Bring to a boil over medium-high heat and cook until fork tender. Transfer to a colander to drain.

Melt the butter in a large saucepan over medium heat. Add the olive oil, celery, and leek. Cook until the vegetables are softened, about 5 minutes. Add the garlic and cook for 1 minute. Stir in the flour and cook for 1 minute. Gradually whisk in the stock and 2 cups of the half-and-half until smooth. Stir in the thyme and sage leaves. Gently simmer for 10 minutes to allow the flavors to meld and the sauce to slightly thicken, stirring frequently.

Meanwhile, wash and remove the stems from the mustard greens. Transfer the leaves to a colander to drain. Pat the greens dry with paper towels and cut them into small strips. Set aside.

Stir the Parmesan cheese and pepper into the stock mixture. Season the mixture with salt to taste. Reduce the heat to medium-low and cook until thickened, 15 to 20 minutes, stirring occasionally. (Note: If a thicker consistency is desired, make a cornstarch slurry with 1 tablespoon cornstarch and 1 tablespoon cold water, and stir it into the stock mixture.) Stir in the potatoes, greens, and peas. Cook for 2 minutes, stirring occasionally. Stir in the turkey meat. Remove the thyme sprigs and discard. Divide the mixture between two 9-inch deep-dish pie pans.

Lightly flour a work surface and use a rolling pin to roll each pie dough into a round large enough to cover the pie pans. Place the dough over the filling. Crimp the edges of the dough together to seal. Cut a few slits in the top of each pie. Lightly brush the remaining 1 tablespoon half-and-half over both pies.

Bake the pies for 22 to 24 minutes, until golden brown. Let stand for 5 minutes before serving.

● *Makes 8 to 10 servings.*

Note: Substitute 2 chicken breasts and 2 chicken drumsticks for the turkey if desired.

Chicken Enchilada Stack

One of the regular Sunday dinner dishes that my great-aunt Ilene prepares for our extended family is chicken enchiladas. Rolling forty to fifty tortillas for enchiladas is time-consuming, so I created a new version that saves time and stress in preparation, giving you more time for fellowship! I use corn tortillas, which contain less fat than flour ones, and serve a fresh green tomato sauce, avocado cubes, and cilantro on the side. Using corn tortillas instead of flour makes the dish a great gluten-free menu option.

1 teaspoon extra-virgin olive oil, plus more for greasing

1 (2-pound) rotisserie chicken

1 teaspoon garlic powder

1 teaspoon onion powder

1 teaspoon ground cumin

3/4 teaspoon fine sea salt, divided

1/8 teaspoon ground cayenne pepper

10 cups packed finely chopped turnip greens or kale

2 cups chicken stock, divided

18 small white corn tortillas

1 1/4 cups shredded Colby Jack cheese, divided

1 1/4 cups shredded pepper jack cheese, divided

Southern Verde Sauce (see recipe on page 285)

1/4 cup chopped fresh cilantro for garnish

1 avocado, pitted and diced, for garnish

Preheat the oven to 375 degrees F. Lightly grease a 9 x 13-inch glass baking dish with olive oil.

Shred both the white and dark meat from the chicken into a medium bowl.

In a small bowl, mix together the garlic powder, onion powder, cumin, 1/4 teaspoon of the sea salt, and cayenne. Pour over the chicken and toss to coat.

In a large sauté pan, heat 1 teaspoon olive oil over medium-high heat. Add the turnip greens and cook, stirring often, until the greens begin to wilt, about 3 minutes. Add 1/2 cup of the chicken stock and the remaining 1/2 teaspoon sea salt. Cook for another 7 minutes.

Heat the remaining 1 1/2 cups chicken stock in a medium saucepan over medium heat. Dip the tortillas, one at a time, into the stock and then place in the baking dish until the bottom of the pan is covered by slightly overlapping tortillas. Sprinkle half of the chicken mixture over the tortillas, then evenly top with half of the turnip greens. Scatter 1/2 cup of the Colby Jack and 1/2 cup of the pepper jack cheese over the turnip greens. Dip more tortillas into the stock and place on top of the cheese. Spread the remaining chicken mixture on top, and scatter 1/2 cup Colby Jack and 1/2 cup pepper jack cheese over the chicken. Place a final layer of dipped tortillas on top of the cheese. Cover the dish with aluminum foil and bake for 15 minutes.

Remove the pan from the oven and pour 1 1/2 cups of the Southern Verde Sauce over the stack. Sprinkle the remaining 1/4 cup Colby Jack and remaining 1/4 cup pepper jack cheese on top. Return to the oven and bake, uncovered, for 5 minutes or until the cheese has melted.

Serve warm topped with the chopped cilantro and avocado. Serve the remaining Southern Verde Sauce on the side.

● *Makes 8 to 10 servings.*

Smoked Red Beans and Rice

This New Orleans–style red beans and rice recipe is uniquely flavored with a touch of smoked salt and ground beef. On many a Sunday, my great-aunt Ilene's stovetop has been covered with huge pots of rice, beans, and greens, enough to feed fifty hungry souls. I love the extra flavor that the ground beef adds to this otherwise classic bean recipe.

1 pound ground beef

1 (7-ounce) smoked andouille sausage, thinly sliced

1/4 cup very finely chopped yellow onion

1/2 celery rib, very finely chopped

1/4 cup very finely chopped green bell pepper

2 cloves garlic, minced

6 cups beef stock, divided

1 (1-pound) package dried red kidney beans, rinsed, drained, and soaked overnight

2 bay leaves

2 sprigs fresh thyme

1 teaspoon smoked salt

1/2 teaspoon fine sea salt

1/4 teaspoon cracked black pepper

1/8 teaspoon smoked paprika

Pinch of cayenne pepper

8 cups cooked long-grain white rice

Chopped fresh chives for garnish

Place the ground beef in a Dutch oven or large pot and cook over medium-high heat until browned, using a spoon to break up the meat as it cooks. Using a slotted spoon, transfer the beef to a plate. Discard the fat. Add the sliced sausage to the pan and cook over medium to medium-high heat until the meat is done and the fat has been rendered. Reduce the heat to medium. Add the onion, celery, and green pepper and cook until the vegetables are translucent, about 6 minutes. Stir in the garlic and cook for 1 minute. Return the ground beef to the pan. Add 4 cups of the beef stock, beans, bay leaves, thyme, smoked salt, sea salt, black pepper, paprika, and cayenne. Increase the heat to medium-high and bring the mixture to a boil. Reduce the heat to medium-low and simmer, uncovered, for 30 minutes. Increase the heat to medium, cover, and cook for 2 1/2 hours, stirring occasionally and adding more stock as needed to keep the beans covered. Cook until the beans are tender. Serve warm over rice. Garnish with chives.

◉ *Makes 6 to 8 servings.*

Roasted-Braised Chicken

Want a delectable chicken recipe that delivers in taste as well as presentation? I created this one for an event where I needed to serve a crowd. The roasting creates a golden brown skin, and the braising ensures that the chicken is moist. Adding vegetables, such as potatoes and carrots, can transform this dish into a one-pot dinner.

1 (5-pound) whole chicken	10 fresh sage leaves
2 celery ribs, roughly chopped	1 tablespoon fine sea salt
1 small onion, sliced	1/4 teaspoon cracked black pepper
7 cloves garlic, smashed	1 tablespoon butter, softened
2 sprigs fresh rosemary	1/2 cup dry white wine
10 sprigs fresh thyme	1 cup low-sodium chicken stock

Preheat the oven to 425 degrees F.

Remove the chicken giblets. Use poultry shears to cut the backbone out of the chicken. Reserve the backbone and giblets to make gravy for another use.

Turn the chicken skin side up and press down on the breastbone to flatten. Pat the outside skin dry with paper towels.

Place the celery, onion, garlic, rosemary, thyme, and sage in a 9 x 13-inch glass baking dish or shallow casserole dish. Place the chicken on top of the vegetables. Combine the salt and pepper in a small bowl. Gently slide your fingers between the meat and skin of the chicken. Separate as much of the skin from the meat as you can. Season with half of the salt and pepper mixture by grabbing pinches of the seasoning, pushing it beneath the skin, and rubbing it onto the meat. Rub the butter over the skin. Sprinkle the remaining seasoning over the skin. Pour the white wine and chicken stock into the dish.

Place the pan on the top rack of the oven and bake for 55 to 65 minutes, until a meat thermometer inserted into the thickest part of the breast reaches 165 degrees F.

Transfer the chicken to a cutting board and let stand for 10 minutes.

Strain the juices through a mesh strainer into a medium saucepan. Skim off the top layer of fat and discard. Season with salt to taste. Cook over medium-high heat until slightly reduced.

Slice the chicken breast. Serve the chicken slices and pieces with the pan sauce.

○ *Makes 5 to 6 servings.*

Shrimp and Andouille Gumbo

My great-grandmother Strahan was known for her shrimp and sausage gumbo. I remember one occasion when she served it in her fine china gumbo bowls. She always prepared her creamy potato salad and had plenty of saltine crackers alongside. Making only a few changes to her original recipe, I updated this classic with spicy andouille sausage and roasted okra.

2 pounds unpeeled large fresh shrimp

16 cups water, divided

2 fresh bay leaves

6 cloves garlic, divided

12 ounces smoked andouille sausage

2 cups finely chopped yellow onion (about 1 medium onion)

2 celery ribs, finely chopped (about 3/4 cups)

1 small green bell pepper, finely chopped (about 1 cup)

1 pound (about 4) small blue crabs

1 tablespoon gumbo filé

2 tablespoons plus 2 1/8 teaspoons fine sea salt, divided

1 (28-ounce) can whole peeled tomatoes, drained

1 1/2 cups canola oil

3 cups all-purpose flour

1/4 teaspoon cracked black pepper

1 1/2 teaspoons crab boil seasoning

1 teaspoon dried parsley

25 small fresh okra, trimmed and cut into 1/2-inch pieces

3/4 teaspoon olive oil

12 cups cooked long-grain white rice, for serving

Peel and devein the shrimp, reserving the shells. Place the shrimp in a bowl and refrigerate. Put the shells in a large pot. Add 12 cups water, the bay leaves, and 4 cloves garlic. Bring to a boil over high heat. Reduce the heat to medium-low and cook for 45 minutes. Skim off any scum that rises to the surface.

While the shrimp stock is cooking, cut the sausage into halves lengthwise and then into 1/4-inch-thick slices. Place the sausage slices in a 10-inch cast-iron skillet and cook over medium heat until browned, 8 to 10 minutes. Transfer the sausage slices to a paper towel-lined plate to drain. Wipe the skillet clean.

Strain the shrimp stock through a mesh strainer into a large bowl. Discard the shells, bay leaves, and garlic. Wash the pot clean of any shell pieces. Return the stock to the pot. Add the onion, celery, and green pepper. Using a fine grater or zester, grate the remaining 2 cloves garlic into the pot. Add the crabs, remaining 4 cups water, filé, and 1 teaspoon salt. Crush the tomatoes in your hand and then add to the pot. Cook over medium-low heat for 30 minutes.

Heat the oil in the skillet over medium heat. Gradually whisk in the flour. Cook for 10 minutes, whisking constantly. Increase the heat to medium-high and cook, whisking constantly, until the mixture reaches a dark brown color, about 25 minutes. Be careful not to burn the flour. If the roux is browning too fast, decrease the heat to medium. Once the roux reaches the color of chocolate, carefully add it to the stock and quickly stir it into the mixture until combined. Add the cooked sausage slices, 2 tablespoons plus 1 teaspoon salt, and pepper. Cook for an additional 15 minutes. Reduce the heat to medium-low and cook for 10 minutes. Add the shrimp, crab boil seasoning, and parsley. Cook for another 10 minutes.

Preheat the oven to 400 degrees F.

Toss the okra with the olive oil and remaining ⅛ teaspoon salt on a baking sheet. Bake for 15 to 17 minutes, until tender. Add the okra to the gumbo. Serve warm over the cooked rice.

▶ *Makes about 12 servings.*

Note: Filé is optional in this recipe. My great-grandmother Strahan didn't use it, but her daughter Ilene incorporates it into her gumbo, and I have as well.

Gumbo at my great-grandmother's house with family and friends.

My great-grandmother peeling shrimp.

Company's Comin'

M ake time for entertaining! Don't wait for a special occasion to fellowship with friends and family. My great-grandma Strahan entertained often and creatively used pantry staples to make everyday meals that satisfied not only family but company as well. Following her example, I created these Company's Comin' recipes that will make entertaining a little easier for you. Make a roast company-ready by cutting and serving individual portions. Dress up meatloaf with a caramelized onion–red wine jus. Set up a food bar with uncooked vegetables and meats, and let guests have fun cooking their own meal with my Southern Hot Pot. What could be easier?

Southern Hot Pot

Mushroom Meatloaf with Caramelized Onion–Red Wine Jus

Mississippi Fried Chicken

Spiced Lamb Kabobs with Mustard Greens–Feta Pesto

Vegan Mushroom "Meatloaf"

Sweet Corn Grit Tamales with Barbecue
Shrimp and Corn Salad

Not Your Grandma's Roast

Pan-Seared Salmon with Persimmon Rum Sauce

Corn Bisque with Shrimp and Grits Croutons

Venison Char Siu

Pan-Seared Rib-Eye Steaks with a
Mushroom Reduction Sauce

Southern Hot Pot

Platters filled with fresh raw vegetables and meats, sliced paper thin, were carefully arranged fondue style around the large pot of boiling stock located on the burner in the center of the table. Fascinated, I watched as my Chinese host instructed me in the ways of eating hot pot. This was definitely a fun experience that I wanted to bring home. I was excited to share the idea with my friends and family, but, of course, I had to put my Southern spin on it, including vegetables such as fresh turnip green leaves, halved Brussels sprouts, and sweet potato slices, and adding venison to the meat selection.

Homemade Chicken Stock

8 pounds bone-in dark meat chicken pieces

4 small yellow onions, peeled and quartered

8 celery ribs, cut crosswise into quarters

8 small carrots, peeled and cut crosswise into quarters

4 cloves garlic, peeled and smashed

16 sprigs fresh thyme

16 bay leaves

Fine sea salt, to taste

1 teaspoon grated ginger, optional

Southern Soy Sauce

1/2 cup Worcestershire sauce

6 tablespoons low-sodium soy sauce

3/4 cup water

2 teaspoons fresh lemon juice

1 teaspoon minced garlic

1 teaspoon grated ginger

Horseradish Cream Sauce

1 1/2 cups sour cream or plain Greek yogurt

1 teaspoon to 1 tablespoon prepared horseradish

Hot Pot

1 (1/2-pound) pork tenderloin

1 (1/2-pound) bottom round beef

1 (1/2-pound) venison filet

1 (6-ounce) andouille sausage or spicy sausage link, cut diagonally into 1/2-inch slices

2 medium sweet potatoes, sliced 1/4 inch thick

2 cups small Brussels sprouts, cut into halves

1 large eggplant, peeled and sliced 1/4 inch thick

2 packages enoki mushrooms, trimmed and pulled apart

1 (8-ounce) container baby bella mushrooms, cleaned and cut into quarters

1 pound baby bok choy

1 bunch turnip green leaves, stems removed

8 ounces vermicelli rice noodles

Sweet chili sauce

To make the chicken stock, divide the chicken, vegetables, and herbs between 2 large pots. Add enough cold water to barely cover the ingredients. Bring to a low boil over medium-high heat. Reduce the heat to medium-low and simmer uncovered for 4 hours. Season with salt to taste. During the cooking, skim off any scum or fat that rises to the surface. Strain the stock through a fine mesh strainer into a large container.

To make the soy sauce, in a small bowl mix together the Worcestershire sauce, soy sauce, water, lemon juice, garlic, and ginger. Store in the refrigerator until ready to serve. The sauce will keep refrigerated in an airtight container for 1 week.

To make the horseradish sauce, in a small bowl mix the sour cream with horseradish to desired taste and pungency. Refrigerate until ready to serve.

To make the hot pot, cut the pork, beef, and venison into paper-thin slices. To make slicing easier, freeze the meats for 1 to 2 hours before slicing or have your butcher slice the meats for you. Arrange the pork, beef, venison, and sausage slices on large plates. On one or more plates, arrange the vegetables and noodles.

Place an electric fondue pot, skillet, or wok in the center of a table. I recommend 1 pot per 3 to 4 people. Pour the Homemade Chicken Stock into the pot(s) and bring to a low boil on a medium to medium-high setting.

Have guests use chopsticks or small tongs to cook their meats and vegetables in the stock. The pork, beef, and venison slices will take 2 to 3 minutes to cook. The sausage will take 4 to 5 minutes. The sweet potatoes and Brussels sprouts will take 5 to 6 minutes. The eggplant, mushrooms, bok choy, and turnip greens will take 3 to 4 minutes to cook. Add the noodles last and cook until soft. A small strainer with a bamboo handle (known as a "spider") is ideal for retrieving any stray meats, vegetables, and noodles from the stock. Any additional stock in the pot can be ladled into guests' bowls along with the noodles to enjoy as a soup. Serve with sweet chili sauce, Southern Soy Sauce, and Horseradish Cream Sauce for dipping.

◗ *Makes 5 to 6 servings of Hot Pot, 10 cups of Homemade Chicken Stock, 1 1/2 cups of Southern Soy Sauce, and 1 cup of Horseradish Cream Sauce.*

Notes: You can find enoki mushrooms at your local Asian grocery store. For the chili sauce, I like to use Mae Ploy's Sweet Chili Sauce. If you don't want to make the Homemade Chicken Stock, use a good-quality packaged broth instead.

Mushroom Meatloaf with Caramelized Onion–Red Wine Jus

In my family, comforting meatloaf is usually served on weekdays for a quick family meal. In this elevated meatloaf, a rich caramelized onion–red wine reduction sauce that is served alongside replaces the usual sweet tomato topping. It's so good it just might replace your weekend steak night dinner.

Mushroom Spread

3 tablespoons butter, divided

1/4 cup very finely chopped leek (white part only)

1 clove garlic, minced

1 (12-ounce) package baby bella mushrooms, roughly chopped

4 ounces shiitake mushrooms, roughly chopped

1 tablespoon finely chopped fresh flat-leaf parsley

1/2 teaspoon fresh thyme leaves

Fine sea salt, to taste

1/8 teaspoon cracked black pepper

Meatloaf

1 1/4 pounds ground chuck

1 1/4 pounds ground beef

5 tablespoons bread crumbs

1/2 teaspoon dried Italian seasoning

1/2 teaspoon fine sea salt

1/8 teaspoon cracked black pepper

1/4 cup whole milk

2 large eggs, beaten

Caramelized Onion–Red Wine Jus

1 tablespoon extra-virgin olive oil

3/4 cup finely chopped yellow onion

Pinch of sugar

1/2 cup finely chopped carrot

1/3 cup finely chopped celery

1 tablespoon minced garlic

1 tablespoon tomato paste

1 1/4 cups red wine

3 cups beef stock

2 sprigs fresh thyme

1/4 teaspoon cracked black pepper

Honey, optional

1 tablespoon cornstarch

1 tablespoon water

To make the spread, heat a medium sauté pan over medium heat. Melt 2 tablespoons of the butter in the pan. Add the leek and garlic. Cook the vegetables until soft, about 4 minutes. Add the remaining 1 tablespoon butter, baby bella mushrooms, and shiitake mushrooms. Cover and cook for 10 minutes. Increase the heat to medium-high and cook, uncovered, until the liquid has evaporated, about 3 minutes. Add the parsley, thyme, salt, and pepper. Stir to combine. Let cool completely. Use immediately or store in an airtight container in the refrigerator for up to 3 days.

To make the meatloaf, preheat the oven to 350 degrees F.

In a large bowl combine the ground chuck and beef. Sprinkle the bread crumbs, Italian seasoning, salt, and pepper over the meat. Pour the milk over the bread crumbs to soften. Add the beaten eggs and gently stir to combine. Transfer half of the meat mixture to an 8 1/2 x 4 1/2-inch glass or metal loaf pan, and then top with the Mushroom Spread. Add the rest of the meat mixture on top.

Bake for about 55 minutes, until the meat is done and the juices run clear. Pour off the fat.

While the meatloaf is cooking, make the Caramelized Onion–Red Wine Jus. Place the olive oil in a medium saucepan. Add the onion and cook over medium-low heat for 10 minutes. Sprinkle a pinch of sugar over the onion to increase caramelization. Cook for another 10 minutes. Add the carrot and celery and cook for 5 minutes. Stir in the garlic and cook for 2 minutes. Stir in the tomato paste and cook for another 2 minutes. Pour the red wine into the pan and cook until reduced by half. Add the beef stock, thyme, and black pepper. Cook for 30 minutes over medium-low to medium heat. Strain the sauce through a mesh strainer, skim off any liquid fat, and discard the solids. Return the sauce to the pan and add honey to taste for a touch of sweetness. In a small bowl mix together the cornstarch and water. Pour into the sauce, stirring constantly until thickened. Season the sauce with salt to taste. Keep warm over low heat until ready to use.

Slice the meatloaf and serve with the warm Caramelized Onion–Red Wine Jus.

◗ *Makes 6 servings and 3 1/2 cups of Caramelized Onion–Red Wine Jus.*

Mississippi Fried Chicken

I had never deep-fried anything before creating this fried chicken recipe. I discovered while testing the recipe for a Southern promotional event at St. Regis Hotel in China that there is an art to frying. I wanted to give everyone a real taste of the South: grits, greens, and fried chicken.

4 boneless, skinless chicken breasts
   (about 2 pounds)
1 1/2 teaspoons fine sea salt, divided
1 1/2 cups buttermilk
1 1/2 cups all-purpose flour
1 teaspoon garlic powder

1 teaspoon onion powder
1/2 teaspoon cracked black pepper
1/2 teaspoon dried thyme
1/8 teaspoon cayenne pepper
1 large egg
1 (48-ounce) bottle canola oil

Place the chicken breasts between 2 sheets of heavy-duty plastic wrap and flatten to 1/2 inch thick using a meat mallet. Sprinkle the chicken breasts with 1/2 teaspoon of the salt and place in an airtight container. Pour the buttermilk over the chicken, cover, and refrigerate for 2 to 4 hours.

In a shallow bowl, combine the remaining 1 teaspoon salt, flour, garlic powder, onion powder, black pepper, thyme, and cayenne.

In another shallow bowl, beat the egg and add 1/4 cup of the buttermilk mixture from the chicken marinade.

Remove the chicken from the buttermilk and shake off the excess. Dip the chicken in the egg mixture and then coat in the flour mixture. Transfer the chicken to a waxed paper lined-baking sheet and let stand for 10 minutes. Reserve the flour mixture.

Meanwhile, heat the oil in a large cast-iron skillet over medium-high heat until the temperature reaches 325 degrees F.

Dredge 2 of the chicken breasts in the seasoned flour again. Shake off the excess and place in the hot oil. Fry for 3 to 4 minutes. Carefully flip the chicken over and fry another 3 to 4 minutes. Maintain the temperature by adjusting the heat as necessary. Place the chicken on a brown paper bag–lined baking sheet to drain. Repeat with remaining chicken breasts. Serve immediately.

● *Makes 4 servings.*

Spiced Lamb Kabobs with Mustard Greens–Feta Pesto

My first introduction to lamb was on a trip to Dubai. My mom and I enjoyed a meal of skewered meats, hummus, and vegetables as we sat on ruby red pillows under a tent in the sand. It was a night to remember! Enjoy these lamb kabobs with grilled naan bread.

Mustard Greens–Feta Pesto

11 mustard green leaves, ribs removed, cut into strips

1 1/2 tablespoons chopped raw shelled pistachios

1 clove garlic, peeled

1/4 teaspoon fine sea salt

4 tablespoons extra-virgin olive oil

1 1/2 tablespoons crumbled feta cheese

1/8 teaspoon finely grated lemon zest

Spiced Lamb Kabobs

1 tablespoon stone-ground mustard

1 teaspoon chopped fresh dill

1 tablespoon chopped fresh cilantro

1/4 teaspoon ground thyme

1/8 teaspoon finely grated lemon zest

2 cloves garlic, minced

3 tablespoons extra-virgin olive oil, divided

3/4 teaspoon fine sea salt, divided

1/2 teaspoon cracked black pepper, divided

2 pounds leg of lamb, cut into 1-inch cubes

1 eggplant, peeled and cut into 1-inch cubes

1 red onion, cut into wedges

To make the pesto, place the mustard greens in a food processor. Add the pistachios, garlic, salt, and olive oil. Process until the mixture begins to form a paste, about 2 minutes. Add the feta cheese and lemon zest. Pulse a few times. Season the pesto to taste with additional salt. Transfer the pesto to a small bowl and use immediately, or store in an airtight container in the refrigerator for up to 2 days.

To make the kabobs, mix together the mustard, dill, cilantro, thyme, lemon zest, garlic, 1 tablespoon of the olive oil, 1/2 teaspoon of the salt, and 1/4 teaspoon of the pepper in a mortar and pestle or food processor. Grind or process into a paste.

Place the lamb in a large zip-top plastic bag and add the herb paste. Close and shake to coat the lamb. Refrigerate for 2 to 4 hours.

Remove the lamb from the refrigerator and let stand until it reaches room temperature, about 30 minutes.

Place the remaining 1/4 teaspoon salt, remaining 1/4 teaspoon pepper, and remaining 2 tablespoons olive oil in a medium bowl. Stir until blended. Add the eggplant and red onion and toss until well coated. Skewer the marinated lamb, eggplant, and red onion alternately on metal or bamboo skewers.

Heat a grill pan over medium heat. Lightly oil the pan and add the kabobs. Cook for about 7 minutes, turning to cook on all sides, until the lamb is medium-rare to medium. Serve warm with the Mustard Greens–Feta Pesto.

◉ *Makes 4 servings and 1 cup of Mustard Greens–Feta Pesto.*

Notes: If using wooden skewers, soak them in water 30 minutes before skewering the meat and vegetables. To grill outdoors, prepare the coals on a charcoal grill. When the coals are glowing and covered in ash, lightly oil the grill grates and place the kabobs on the grates. Cook for 8 to 10 minutes, turning to cook on all sides, until the lamb is medium-rare to medium.

Vegan Mushroom "Meatloaf"

My vegan meatloaf is very "meaty." The hearty mushrooms and butter beans lend a meat-like texture to this dish. It's an entrée that not only vegans and vegetarians will rave over but meat eaters as well. Just don't tell the meat eaters that there is no meat in the dish until after they've told you how great it is!

Mushroom–Red Wine Jus

1 (5-ounce) package dried baby bella mushrooms

4 cups plus 1/2 tablespoon water, divided

1/2 tablespoon extra-virgin olive oil

1/3 cup finely chopped yellow onion

Pinch of sugar

1/4 cup finely chopped carrot

1/4 cup finely chopped celery

1/2 tablespoon minced garlic

1/2 tablespoon tomato paste

3/4 cup red wine

1 sprig fresh thyme

1/8 teaspoon cracked black pepper

Honey, optional

1/2 tablespoon cornstarch

Vegan Mushroom "Meatloaf"

1 (8-ounce) package fresh baby bella mushrooms, coarsely chopped

1 (9 1/2-ounce) package king trumpet mushrooms, coarsely chopped

1 tablespoon plus 1 teaspoon extra-virgin olive oil, divided

1/4 cup finely chopped yellow onion

2 cloves garlic, minced

1 (16-ounce) can butter beans, drained and rinsed

1/4 cup vegetable stock, plus more for processing

2 teaspoons tahini

2 tablespoons finely chopped sun-dried tomatoes packed in oil

1/2 teaspoon stone-ground mustard

1 tablespoon soy sauce

1 tablespoon vegan Worcestershire sauce

1/2 teaspoon fresh thyme leaves

1/2 teaspoon sea salt

1/8 teaspoon smoked salt

1/4 teaspoon cracked black pepper

1/2 cup panko bread crumbs

Liquid egg replacer for 1 egg

To make the Mushroom–Red Wine Jus, place the mushrooms in a medium saucepan. Add 4 cups of the water. Bring to a boil over medium-high heat. Reduce the heat to medium-low and cook, covered, for 15 minutes. Strain the mushroom liquid through a fine mesh strainer into a bowl. Reserve the mushrooms for another use. Set aside the liquid.

Heat the olive oil in a medium saucepan over medium-low heat. Add the onion and cook for 10 minutes. Sprinkle a pinch of sugar over the onion to increase caramelization. Cook for another 10 minutes. Add the carrot and celery and cook for 5 minutes. Stir in the garlic and cook for 2 minutes. Stir in the tomato paste and cook for 2 minutes. Add the red wine and cook until reduced by half. Add the reserved mushroom stock, thyme, and black pepper. Cook for 30 minutes over medium-low to medium heat. Strain the sauce through a wire mesh strainer into a bowl and then return the liquid to the pan. Add honey to taste for a touch of sweetness. Mix together the cornstarch and remaining $1/2$ tablespoon water in a small bowl. Add to the sauce, stirring constantly until thickened. Season the sauce with salt to taste.

To make the mushroom loaf, preheat the oven to 350 degrees F. Grease three 5 $3/4$ x 3 x 2-inch mini loaf pans.

Place half of the baby bella and king trumpet mushrooms in the bowl of a food processor, and pulse until finely chopped. Place the chopped mushrooms in a medium sauté pan. Repeat with the other half of the mushrooms. Add 1 tablespoon of the olive oil to the pan. Cook over medium heat until the liquid from the mushrooms has evaporated, about 10 minutes, stirring occasionally. Spoon the mixture into a bowl.

Wipe the pan clean with a paper towel. Add the remaining 1 teaspoon olive oil to the pan. Add the onion and cook for 4 minutes over medium heat. Add the garlic, beans, and stock. Cover and cook over medium heat until the beans are soft, about 8 minutes. Transfer the bean mixture to the bowl of a food processor. Add a splash of vegetable stock and the tahini, and process until smooth.

Combine the bean mixture, sun-dried tomatoes, and mushroom mixture in a large bowl. Add the mustard, soy sauce, Worcestershire sauce, thyme, salt, smoked salt, and pepper. Mix well. Stir in the panko and egg replacer until well mixed. Spoon 1 $1/2$ cups of the mixture into each of 2 loaf pans. Place the remaining mixture in the third pan. (It will be only half full.) Gently press the mixture down in the pans.

Bake for about 30 minutes. Let stand for 5 minutes, then transfer the mini loaves to a serving plate. Serve with the Mushroom–Red Wine Jus.

▶ *Makes 4 to 5 servings and about 4 cups of Mushroom–Red Wine Jus.*

Notes: Dried baby bella mushrooms (used in the Mushroom–Red Wine Jus) are sometimes labeled crimini. King trumpet mushrooms can be found at your local Asian grocery store. For a vegetarian version, use 1 large egg for liquid egg replacer.

Sweet Corn Grit Tamales with Barbecue Shrimp and Corn Salad

Typical Mississippi Delta tamales are made with cornmeal, unlike the Mexican masa variety. My own Southern version uses grits enhanced with the flavor of sweet corn. Using grits enables me to shorten the cooking time and to lighten up the tamale by not using fat. To serve, top with spiced-up Barbecue Shrimp and Corn Salad. These tamales are perfect for summer gatherings.

Grit Tamales

3 ears of corn, husks and silk removed
1 cup half-and-half
4 1/2 cups water

25 dried corn husks
1 1/2 cups yellow quick-cooking stone-ground grits
1 1/2 teaspoons fine sea salt

Corn Salad

4 ears of corn, husks and silk removed
2 teaspoons chopped cilantro leaves
1 teaspoon very finely chopped jalapeño pepper
2 teaspoons chopped pimientos

2 1/4 teaspoons rice vinegar
4 1/2 teaspoons extra-virgin olive oil
1/4 teaspoon fine sea salt
1/4 teaspoon cracked black pepper

Barbecue Shrimp

2 teaspoons Worcestershire powder
2 teaspoons garlic powder
1 teaspoon onion powder
3/4 teaspoon fine sea salt
1/4 teaspoon cracked black pepper

1/8 teaspoon finely grated lemon zest
Pinch of cayenne pepper
2 pounds large shrimp, peeled and deveined
1 tablespoon butter
1 teaspoon extra-virgin olive oil

To make the tamales, cut the corn kernels from the cobs with a paring knife. Reserve the cobs. Place the kernels and half-and-half in a medium saucepan. Cover and cook over medium-low heat for 35 minutes, stirring occasionally. Uncover and cook for an additional 5 minutes. Transfer to the bowl of a food processor and process until smooth.

Meanwhile, place the cobs in a medium saucepan with 4 1/2 cups water. Cover and cook for 40 minutes over medium-low heat. Discard the cobs.

Soak the corn husks in warm water for 30 minutes.

Bring the corn stock to a boil over medium-high heat. Whisk in the grits and salt until incorporated. Reduce the heat and cook until the grits are tender, following the instructions on the package. Remove the pan from the heat and stir in the corn puree.

Rinse and clean the corn husks thoroughly. Drain well and pat dry. Cut 20 long strips out of a few husks.

Spoon 1/2 cup of the grits mixture into the center of the smooth side of a husk. Tightly fold one side in, then pull the other side over. Tightly twist each end together and secure by tying with a husk strip. Repeat with the rest of the grits mixture until 10 tamales are made.

Place the tamales in a bamboo steamer (or in a pasta insert or colander over a pot with 2 inches of water in it). Cover and steam the tamales over medium-low heat for about 25 minutes.

To make the salad, cut the corn kernels off the cobs with a paring knife and place in a medium bowl. Add the cilantro leaves, jalapeño, and pimientos.

In a small bowl whisk the rice vinegar, olive oil, salt, and pepper until well blended. Pour over the corn mixture and toss to combine. Season with additional salt to taste. Refrigerate until ready to use.

To make the shrimp, mix together the Worcestershire powder, garlic powder, onion powder, salt, black pepper, lemon zest, and cayenne in a medium bowl. Toss the shrimp in the seasoning mixture until coated.

Heat a large cast-iron skillet over medium to medium-high heat. Add the butter and olive oil. Once the butter has melted, add the shrimp. Do not overcrowd the skillet. Cook in batches if the shrimp cannot evenly fit in the bottom of the skillet. Cook the shrimp until just barely opaque throughout, 2 to 3 minutes per side.

To assemble, place a tamale on a plate and untie and unwrap it. Top with some of the Barbecue Shrimp and Corn Salad. Serve immediately.

⬤ *Makes 10 servings.*

Notes: You can find dried corn husks in the international aisle of your grocery store. If you cannot find quick-cooking stone-ground grits, regular stone-ground grits can be substituted. Cooking time will increase. Worcestershire powder can be found online and at specialty kitchen or spice stores.

Not Your Grandma's Roast

I've elevated my great-grandmother Strahan's roast by cutting it into individual portions before cooking it in a slow cooker. This is a great, inexpensive way to feed several of your friends and family on the weekend, and it's almost completely hands-free.

1 (4-pound) bottom round roast
2 tablespoons fine sea salt
1 teaspoon cracked black pepper
2 celery ribs, roughly chopped
1 yellow onion, sliced

4 cloves garlic, thinly sliced
1 tablespoon soy sauce
1 tablespoon Worcestershire sauce
1 1/4 cups beef stock

Remove the layer of fat from the bottom side of the roast in one piece if possible. Set aside.

Cut the beef into 7 equal portions and place them in the bottom of a 6-quart slow cooker.

In a small bowl mix together the salt and pepper. Rub the seasoning over the meat.

Add the celery, onion, garlic, soy sauce, Worcestershire sauce, and beef stock to the slow cooker. Place the layer of fat on top of the meat. Cover and cook on low for 8 hours. Turn the heat off and let stand for 30 minutes. Discard the layer of fat.

Transfer the beef to a serving dish. Working in batches, transfer the vegetables to a fine mesh strainer over a bowl. With the back of a spoon, press the vegetables against the strainer to release any cooking liquid. Discard the vegetables. Spoon the layer of fat from the top of the liquid. Blend the cooking liquid in a blender until smooth, then pour half of the liquid over the beef. Serve over mashed potatoes or rice with the remaining pan juices.

Makes 7 servings.

Pan-Seared Salmon with Persimmon Rum Sauce

The fall season in the South is marked more by football games and tailgating than by falling leaves and changing colors. In most parts of the South, true fall weather doesn't start until late October, but when it happens, the cooler temperatures make for a perfect afternoon walk around the neighborhood. On one such family outing, I discovered a wild persimmon tree near my house, its limbs bearing the small bright orange fruits and the ground underneath liberally scattered with the softened darker orange ones. My mom warned me that the pretty ones on the tree were not ripe and too bitter to eat, but the mushy ones on the ground were sweet treats. After one taste, I had to agree and began concocting all kinds of persimmon recipes in my mind. One of the results, a delicious Persimmon Rum Sauce, can be served warm atop my sister Brittyn's favorite fish, seared salmon. The contrast of sweet, tangy, and a touch of saltiness makes for a mouthwatering salmon dish.

Persimmon Rum Sauce

3 large very ripe persimmons
2/3 cup water
1/4 cup low-sodium soy sauce
1/2 cup firmly packed light brown sugar
1 1/2 tablespoons fresh orange juice

1 tablespoon butter
1/4 cup finely chopped yellow onion
1/2 head Roasted Garlic (see recipe on page 290)
1 tablespoon dark rum

Pan-Seared Salmon

4 (6-ounce) skinless center-cut salmon fillets

1/2 teaspoon fine sea salt
2 teaspoons canola oil

To make the sauce, wash the persimmons and cut off the green tops. Place a wire mesh strainer over a 4-cup measuring cup. One at a time, press the persimmons against the strainer to release the pulp. Discard the seeds and skins.

Combine the water, persimmon pulp, soy sauce, brown sugar, and orange juice in a medium saucepan over medium-high heat. Bring to a boil, then reduce the heat to low and simmer.

In a small sauté pan, melt the butter. Add the onion. Squeeze the pulp from 1/2 head Roasted Garlic into the pan. Cook until the onions are translucent, 5 to 7 minutes.

Add the onion mixture to the persimmon mixture and stir until well blended. Stir in the rum. Simmer until the sauce has reduced by about half and thickened, about 45 minutes. Transfer to a half-pint jar.

To make the salmon, pat the salmon fillets dry with paper towels and season with the salt. Heat a 12-inch cast-iron skillet over medium-high heat. Add the oil to the skillet. When the oil is hot and begins to shimmer, add the salmon fillets. Cook for about 4 minutes, then flip and cook for another 3 to 4 minutes. Serve the salmon fillets with the persimmon sauce.

○ *Makes 4 servings and 1 cup of Persimmon Rum Sauce.*

Note: I prefer to use Hachiya persimmons, but you may also use Fuyu.

Corn Bisque with Shrimp and Grits Croutons

I love shrimp and grits! In my first cookbook I created two versions, but I knew I had to feature a version in this cookbook as well. These crispy-coated croutons are served in a creamy corn bisque. The secret to the bisque's intense corn flavor is using the whole corn, from husk to cob.

Grits Croutons

1 1/3 cups water

1 cup whole milk

1 cup stone-ground grits

2 tablespoons butter

1/2 teaspoon fine sea salt

1/4 cup grated Parmesan cheese

Canola oil

1/3 cup fine stone-ground yellow cornmeal

Corn Bisque

6 ears of yellow corn, in the husks

4 cups half-and-half

1 tablespoon butter

1/2 yellow bell pepper, chopped

1/2 yellow onion, chopped

4 small cloves garlic, minced

1 cup heavy cream

Fine sea salt, to taste

Roasted Corn

3 ears of yellow corn, husks and silk removed

1 tablespoon extra-virgin olive oil

1/8 teaspoon fine sea salt

1/4 teaspoon cracked black pepper

Shrimp and Sausage

1 (8-ounce) smoked andouille sausage, cut into halves lengthwise and then diagonally into 1-inch-thick slices

1 pound large shrimp, peeled and deveined

1/4 teaspoon fine sea salt

1/4 teaspoon cracked black pepper

Pinch of cayenne pepper

Chopped fresh chives for garnish

To make the croutons, bring the water and milk to a low boil in a medium saucepan over medium-high heat. Stir in the grits and reduce the heat to low. Cover and cook for about 25 minutes, stirring occasionally. Remove the pan from the heat and stir in the butter, salt, and Parmesan cheese. Cook, uncovered, until tender, about 10 minutes. Line an 8 1/2 x 4 1/2-inch glass or metal loaf pan with plastic wrap. Spoon the grits mixture into the pan and spread evenly. Refrigerate until set, 1 to 2 hours. Once the grits have set, remove from the refrigerator and cut into 1-inch cubes.

Pour the oil into a deep saucepan and heat over medium-high heat. Toss the grits cubes in the cornmeal until coated. Place in the hot oil, a few at a time, and fry until golden brown and crisp. Transfer to a paper towel–lined plate to drain. To keep the croutons warm, transfer to a wire rack–lined baking sheet and place in a 250-degree F oven.

To make the bisque, remove the husks and silk from the corn. Roughly cut the husks into 2- to 3-inch pieces and place in a large pot with the silk. Use a paring knife or corn zipper to remove the kernels from the cobs. Reserve the kernels. Cut the cobs in half and add them to the pot. Pour in the half-and-half. Bring the mixture to a low boil over medium-high heat, then reduce the heat to low, cover, and cook for about 1 hour, stirring occasionally.

Meanwhile, melt the butter in a medium saucepan over medium heat. Add the reserved corn kernels, yellow bell pepper, and onion. Sauté the vegetables for 8 minutes, then add the garlic and cook for another minute. Stir in the heavy cream. Reduce the heat to low and cook until the corn has softened, about 40 minutes. Working in batches, transfer the corn mixture to a blender jar and puree until smooth. Strain over a wire mesh strainer back into the saucepan.

Strain the corncob cream through a fine mesh strainer into a large bowl, pressing the solids to extract as much liquid as possible. Discard the husks, silk, and cob pieces. Stir 1 ¼ cups of the corn cob cream into the corn bisque. To thin the bisque, add more corn cob cream. Season the bisque with salt to taste.

To make the roasted corn, preheat the oven to 400 degrees F. Place the ears of corn on a baking sheet. Drizzle the olive oil over the corn and toss to coat. Season with the salt and pepper. Bake for 20 to 25 minutes. Cut the kernels off the cobs.

To make the shrimp and sausage, cook the sausage until browned, about 5 minutes. Transfer to a paper towel–lined plate to drain. Cover to keep warm. Reserve fat in the pan.

Toss the shrimp with the salt, black pepper, and cayenne in a medium bowl. In the same pan, heat the fat from the sausage over medium-high heat. Add the shrimp and cook for 2 minutes. Flip and cook another minute, or until pink and opaque. Transfer the shrimp to a plate.

To assemble, spoon some of the Corn Bisque into shallow bowls. Top with the Grits Croutons, shrimp, sausage, and roasted corn kernels. Garnish with the chopped chives.

⊙ *Makes 6 servings.*

Venison Char Siu

Char Siu is a popular Cantonese charred roasted pork dish marinated in a sweet and spicy barbecue sauce. This venison version is marinated in a sweet and spicy blackberry sauce and then quickly roasted in a hot oven, producing a thin crust on the outside while still maintaining moisture on the inside. And it's so tender you may not even need a knife to eat it. Get ready to discover your new favorite way to eat venison.

2 cups blackberry preserves
1/4 teaspoon minced garlic
1/4 cup finely chopped red bell pepper
1/4 cup finely chopped red onion

2 teaspoons finely chopped pickled jalapeño peppers
1 1/2 teaspoons balsamic vinegar
1 tablespoon soy sauce
2 (2-pound) venison tenderloins

Combine the preserves, garlic, red bell pepper, onion, jalapeños, and vinegar in a medium saucepan. Bring to a boil over medium-high heat. Reduce the heat to medium and cook for 8 minutes. Reduce the heat to low and cook for 18 to 20 minutes. Remove from the heat and let cool slightly and thicken for 5 minutes.

Combine the blackberry glaze and soy sauce in a blender jar and blend until smooth. In a small bowl reserve a few tablespoons of the glaze to brush on the cooked meat.

Place the tenderloins in a shallow rectangular dish. Pour the glaze mixture over the top and toss to coat. Cover and refrigerate for 2 hours or overnight.

Preheat the oven to 475 degrees F. Line a baking sheet with aluminum foil and top with a wire rack.

Remove the venison tenderloins from the marinade and place on the wire rack. Reserve the marinade. Bake on the top rack of the oven for 15 minutes, basting with the marinade every 5 minutes. Transfer to a cutting board and let stand for 5 minutes. Meanwhile, heat the reserved glaze, brush over the tops of the tenderloins, and slice the meat into about 1-inch-thick slices on a diagonal.

● *Makes 8 servings.*

Note: For a reduced-sugar option, use Blackberry Refrigerator Preserves (see recipe on page 21) in the glaze.

Pan-Seared Rib-Eye Steaks with a Mushroom Reduction Sauce

A meal of meat and potatoes is my dad's favorite. For his birthday dinner every year, instead of dining out, he asks me to prepare a steak dinner. My Smashed Potatoes (see recipe on page 134) are a perfect accompaniment to this steak dish. If you have a meat and potato lover in your family, prepare this special dish for them.

Mushroom Reduction Sauce

3 tablespoons butter, divided

1/4 cup finely chopped yellow onion

1 clove garlic, minced

6 large baby bella mushrooms, cut into 1/2-inch cubes

1 cup beef stock

3 tablespoons Worcestershire sauce

1 tablespoon soy sauce

1/4 teaspoon cracked black pepper

Steaks

4 boneless rib-eye steaks, 1 inch thick (3 pounds total)

2 teaspoons fine sea salt

1/2 teaspoon cracked black pepper

2 tablespoons canola oil, divided

To make the sauce, melt 2 tablespoons of the butter in a 10-inch cast-iron skillet over medium heat. Add the onion and cook until softened, about 6 minutes. Add the garlic and cook for 1 minute. Add the mushrooms and cook for 5 minutes, stirring occasionally. Stir in the beef stock, Worcestershire sauce, soy sauce, and pepper. Cook over medium to medium-high heat until reduced by half, 10 to 15 minutes, stirring occasionally. Stir in the remaining 1 tablespoon butter. Transfer sauce to a medium saucepan and keep warm over low heat. Wipe the skillet clean.

To make the steaks, pat them dry and then season both sides with the salt and pepper. Heat the skillet over medium-high heat. Add 1 tablespoon of the oil. When the oil is shimmering, add 2 of the steaks. (They should sizzle when they hit the pan.) Cook for 3 minutes, then flip and cook for another 2 to 3 minutes for medium. Transfer to a cutting board. Add the remaining 1 tablespoon oil to the pan and the remaining 2 steaks and cook.

To serve, cut the steaks into thin slices or serve whole with the warm Mushroom Reduction Sauce.

◗ *Makes 4 servings.*

Somethin' Sweet

My dad likes to tell stories of how in the good ol' days he or my great-grandpa Strahan cranked the handle of their old green wooden ice cream freezer while aunts, uncles, and cousins sat on the back porch fellowshipping. Now and then, they stopped to add ice and rock salt, and eventually they had ice cream. On a hot summer day, they ladled it into whatever cup or bowl was available and ate it immediately. My recipes rely on electric ice cream freezers, but they're just as delicious as the ones my dad ate at my great-grandmother's house. They may even taste better to him, since he doesn't have to spend all day turning the crank.

Looking for a fun dessert to serve family and friends? My Hello Dolly Ice Cream Sandwiches, Old-Fashioned Fudge Popsicles, and Sweet Tea Peach Cobbler are just a few of the treats in this chapter that will keep everyone coming back for a little somethin' sweet.

Chocolate Ganache

Best Ever Devil's Food Chocolate Cupcakes

Toasted Coconut-Pecan Topping

Dessert Toast

Sweet Tea Peach Cobbler

Baked Apple Hand Pies

Fresh Strawberry Cake

Chocolate-Hazelnut Spread Banana Cobbler

A Little "Nutty" Banana Pudding

Toasted Coconut Cream Pie with Chocolate and Pecans

Oatmeal Lace Cookies

Southern Candy Bar

Blueberry-Pecan Crunch

White Hot Chocolate

Cracker Jack Panna Cotta

Buttermilk Pecan Pralines

Hello Dolly Ice Cream Sandwiches

Mini Lemon Meringue Pies

Mississippi Mud Pie

Gluten-Free Bread Pudding

Old-Fashioned Fudge Popsicles

Caramelized Banana Butter Pecan Cake with Oat-Pecan Crumble

Dark Chocolate Granola

Brownie Cookies

White Chocolate Bread Pudding Beignets

Semi-Frozen Lime Pie with a Graham Brittle Crust

Chocolate Ganache

Chocolate Ganache may be used as a glaze for cupcakes or whipped and used as a frosting.

3 cups heavy cream
24 ounces semisweet chocolate,
    chopped

2 tablespoons strong brewed coffee

Place the cream in a medium saucepan and heat until warm over medium heat.

Place the chocolate in a medium bowl. Pour the warm cream over the chocolate and let stand for 2 minutes. Whisk until smooth. Pour the coffee into the chocolate mixture and whisk to combine. Use immediately as a glaze. Alternatively, make a frosting by letting the ganache cool for about 1 hour at room temperature and then beating it with a hand mixer until light and fluffy.

To glaze cupcakes, dip them into the slightly warm ganache. To frost cupcakes with whipped ganache, spoon the thickened ganache into a gallon-size zip-top freezer bag. Snip a 1/2-inch tip from the corner of the bag. Pipe the whipped ganache onto the cupcakes.

● *Makes about 2 1/2 cups glaze or 5 1/4 cups whipped ganache.*

Note: For a dark chocolate ganache, substitute bittersweet chocolate.

Best Ever Devil's Food Chocolate Cupcakes

My brothers-in-law, Chase and Scott, love cake. Chase has even been known to eat cake for breakfast. These chocolate cupcakes are their favorite, especially when topped with rich chocolate ganache. Now if I can just find a way to keep them out of the cake batter!

1/2 cup unsalted butter, softened
1/4 cup canola oil
2 cups pure cane sugar
2 large eggs
1 large egg yolk
1 teaspoon pure vanilla extract
1 tablespoon strong brewed coffee
1 cup hot water
1/2 cup unsweetened cocoa powder

1 ounce dark chocolate
2 cups all-purpose flour
1 teaspoon baking soda
1/2 teaspoon fine sea salt
1/2 cup buttermilk
Chocolate Ganache (see recipe on page 229) or Toasted Coconut-Pecan Topping (see recipe on page 232)

Preheat the oven to 350 degrees F. Line two 12-cup muffin pans with paper liners.

Place the butter in a mixing bowl and beat with an electric mixer on medium speed until creamy. Add the oil and sugar. Mix until combined. Add the eggs and egg yolk, one at a time, beating after each addition. Add the vanilla and coffee. In a small bowl mix together the hot water, cocoa powder, and chocolate. Add gradually to the batter and beat until blended.

Sift the flour, baking soda, and salt into a bowl. Alternately add the flour mixture and the buttermilk to the batter, beating on low speed until combined after each addition.

Fill each paper liner with about 1/4 cup of the batter. Bake the cupcakes for about 17 minutes, until a wooden pick inserted near the center comes out clean. Transfer the cupcakes to a wire rack and let cool.

Glaze the cupcakes with slightly warm Chocolate Ganache or frost them with whipped ganache or Toasted Coconut-Pecan Topping.

● *Makes 24 cupcakes.*

Toasted Coconut-Pecan Topping

Toasted coconut pairs beautifully with the Devil's Food Chocolate Cupcakes. Try it as an alternative to the Chocolate Ganache.

3 cups sweetened shredded coconut, divided
2 cups coconut milk
2 cups pure cane sugar

6 egg yolks
1 teaspoon pure vanilla extract
2 cups chopped pecans

Preheat the oven to 350 degrees F.

Evenly spread 1 cup of the coconut on a baking sheet and bake for about 5 minutes, until golden brown, stirring halfway through the baking time.

Combine the coconut milk, sugar, and egg yolks in a medium saucepan. Cook over medium heat until thickened and almost coating the back of a spoon, about 15 minutes, whisking constantly. Remove from the heat and stir in the vanilla, toasted coconut, remaining 2 cups shredded coconut, and pecans. Let cool and thicken at room temperature, or spoon into a bowl and refrigerate. Slightly warm the topping before frosting the cupcakes.

To frost the cupcakes, spoon the topping onto the cupcakes. Serve immediately.

▶ *Makes about 5 1/2 cups.*

Note: Use the Toasted Coconut-Pecan Topping as a frosting for carrot, spice, and hummingbird cakes.

Dessert Toast

This grown-up version of cinnamon toast is a simple yet elegant dessert. The traditional white bread slices are replaced with pillowy, toasted slices of angel food cake. The cake slices are then topped with a simple cinnamon butter or one of the nineteen other toppings (see page 235), including an unconventional mint pesto that will make you rethink greens for dessert.

1 box angel food cake mix, plus
   ingredients listed on the box

Cooking spray

Preheat the oven to 350 degrees F.

Follow the package directions to prepare the batter. Lightly grease two 5 1/2 x 3 x 2 1/4-inch mini loaf pans with cooking spray. Fill the mini loaf pans about three-quarters full with the cake batter.

Bake the loaves for 19 to 21 minutes, until browned on top. Remove from the pans and transfer to a wire rack to cool. Repeat with the remaining batter to make a total of 7 mini cake loaves.

Preheat the broiler.

Using a serrated knife, cut each loaf into 7 (1/2-inch-thick) slices. Place the slices on a baking sheet and broil until golden brown.

To assemble, top each slice of toasted angel food cake with one or more desired toppings.

◗ *Makes 7 mini loaves, or 16 servings.*

Notes: I prefer to use Betty Crocker angel food cake mix. For the hazelnut spread, I use Nutella brand.

Toppings for Dessert Toast

Chocolate-hazelnut spread

Chocolate Ganache (page 229)

Homemade Caramel (page 292)

Roasted Peanut Butter (page 284)

Homemade Whipped Cream (page 293)

Blackberry Refrigerator Preserves (page 21)

Fresh Granny Smith apple slices

Fresh banana slices

Cinnamon butter

Persimmon Butter (page 23)

Cookie spread, such as Biscoff European Cookie Spread

Mint Pesto (page 279)

Brie cheese

Goat cheese

Mini marshmallows

Graham cracker crumbs

Sweetened shredded coconut, toasted

Chopped pecans, toasted

Pumpkin seeds

Pomegranate seeds

Take your Dessert Toast toppings a step further and try these combinations:

Apple Pie: apple slices and Homemade Caramel

Mint Delight: Mint Pesto and Brie cheese

S'mores: chocolate-hazelnut spread, graham cracker crumbs, and mini marshmallows

Elvis: Roasted Peanut Butter, banana slices, and Dark Chocolate Ganache

Farm Stand: Persimmon Butter, pumpkin seeds, and pomegranate seeds

Southern Comfort: cookie spread, Chocolate Ganache, pecans, and toasted coconut

Childhood Treat: cinnamon butter

PB&J: Roasted Peanut Butter and Blackberry Refrigerator Preserves

Sweet Tea Peach Cobbler

My family and I were "pickers" long before the show on the History Channel ever became popular. Yard sales and flea markets have always been a part of our family outings. Picking is such an addiction that traveling down the road and spotting a sign for a flea market is cause for an immediate U-turn and an interruption to any plans already on the docket. Taking a day trip to Mobile, Alabama, or the Mississippi Gulf Coast usually includes a trip to the local flea markets, scouting for treasures of vintage jewelry, dishwares, or linens. Amazingly, I have also discovered that they are a great source for all kinds of farm vegetables and fruits in season. In the summer, with visions of warm, crusty peach cobbler and snowy peaks of cream melting and mingling with cinnamon-sweet peaches, I never leave the market without a basket of golden ripe peaches on my arm. I can barely wait until I sink my teeth into a delicate fuzzy-skinned peach, laughing as the juicy goodness escapes in small dribbles down my chin. I try to save at least half of the basket to make sweet treats like this one.

Sweet Tea Peach Cobbler

1 cup water
1 family-size tea bag
1 cup pure cane sugar, divided
1/8 teaspoon ground cinnamon
4 medium peaches, peeled and sliced

1/4 cup (1/2 stick) butter
1 cup self-rising flour
1 cup skim milk
Pinch of ground cinnamon
1 teaspoon pure vanilla extract

Buttermilk Whipped Cream

3/4 cup heavy cream
1/4 cup low-fat buttermilk

3 tablespoons powdered sugar

To make the cobbler, preheat the oven to 350 degrees F.

Bring the water and tea bag to a boil in a medium saucepan over medium-high heat. Boil for 2 minutes. Remove the tea bag and discard. Stir in 1/4 cup of the sugar until dissolved. Cook for another minute. Add the 1/8 teaspoon cinnamon and peach slices. Remove the pan from the heat and let stand for 5 minutes.

Place the butter in a 9-inch cast-iron skillet. Place in the oven to melt.

In a medium bowl combine the flour, remaining 3/4 cup sugar, milk, pinch of cinnamon, and vanilla. Pour the batter into the skillet. Using a spoon, evenly distribute the peach slices and liquid over the batter. Bake for 45 minutes or until golden brown.

To make the whipped cream, beat the cream in a medium bowl using a hand mixer on high speed until thickened. Reduce the speed to low and add the buttermilk. Increase the speed to high and beat until soft peaks form. Beat in the powdered sugar. Use immediately.

Serve the peach cobbler warm with the Buttermilk Whipped Cream.

◐ *Makes 6 to 8 servings of cobbler and 2 cups of Buttermilk Whipped Cream.*

Baked Apple Hand Pies

My great-grandma McCarter was a great sweets cook, and tiny fried apple pies were her specialty. She picked the apples from the tree in her backyard, cooked them down, and then encased them in biscuit dough to fry. Oh my gosh, they were so good! Over the years, my mom has made them for us too. They are one of my favorite treats, and that's why I decided to re-create the recipe using a simple-to-make olive oil pie pastry. I use an apple filling in this recipe, but you can fill your pies with whatever fruit is in season.

1 tablespoon butter

1/2 cup firmly packed light brown sugar

2 large Granny Smith apples, finely chopped (about 2 cups)

1/2 teaspoon ground cinnamon

1 recipe of Olive Oil Pie Dough (see recipe on page 291)

1 large egg, beaten

2 teaspoons pure cane sugar, optional

1/8 teaspoon ground cinnamon, optional

Place the butter in a medium sauté pan and melt it over medium heat. Add the brown sugar and cook until almost dissolved. Add the apple and cinnamon. Stir to combine. Cover and cook until the apples are soft, about 20 minutes. Transfer to the bowl of a food processor. Pulse until the mixture becomes a chunky applesauce consistency. Let cool slightly.

Preheat the oven to 375 degrees F. Lightly grease a baking sheet with cooking spray.

Place the Olive Oil Pie Dough on a lightly floured work surface. Sprinkle a little flour over the dough. Using a floured rolling pin, roll the dough out to a circle about 1/8-inch thick. Using a 4-inch round cutter (I use a wide-mouth mason jar lid), cut the dough into rounds. Form the scraps of dough together and roll out again. Repeat to create a total of 13 rounds.

Roll each round into a 41/2-inch circle. Place about 11/2 tablespoons of the apple mixture on one half of each dough round. Rub some of the beaten egg around the rim of the dough. Fold the dough over and pinch closed. Using a fork dipped in flour, press around the edges of each pie to seal. Place the filled pies on the baking sheet. Lightly brush the tops of the pies with the remaining beaten egg. Sprinkle the cane sugar and 1/8 teaspoon cinnamon on top, if using.

Bake for 18 to 20 minutes, until light golden brown. Transfer to a wire rack and let cool slightly, 3 minutes, before serving.

◉ *Makes 13 servings.*

Fresh Strawberry Cake

||||||||||||||||||||||||||||||||||||||||||||||||||||||||||||||||||||||||||||||||||||||||||||||||||||||||||||||||||||||||||||||||||||||||||||||||||

In parts of the South, it's either the end of winter or spring that brings row after row of bright red strawberries beckoning enticingly from farmers' fields and roadside fruit stands. It also brings an abundance of strawberry desserts. My great-aunt Ilene always makes her famous strawberry cake with strawberry gelatin and fresh strawberries, covered in a deliciously rich homemade strawberry frosting. Each bite is rich with fresh strawberry taste. It doesn't last long. Inspired, I decided to splurge on a full flat of strawberries, plenty to make my own strawberry cake, and a few extra for eating on the ride home. I've replaced the gelatin with natural strawberry spread and lightened up the cake by beating and folding in the egg whites.

Fresh Strawberry Cake
||||||||||||||||||||||||||||||||||||||||||||||||||||||||||||||||

$2/3$ cup butter, softened

$1\,3/4$ cups pure cane sugar

2 large eggs, separated

$1\,1/2$ teaspoons pure vanilla extract

1 cup natural strawberry fruit spread

3 cups sifted all-purpose flour

$1\,1/4$ teaspoons baking soda

$1\,1/4$ cups buttermilk

$1/2$ cup diced strawberries

Strawberry Icing
||||||||||||||||||||||||||||||||||||||||||||||||||

1 cup butter, softened

$7\,1/2$ cups powdered sugar

$3/4$ cup finely chopped strawberries

$1/2$ cup toasted chopped pecans

1 cup sweetened shredded coconut, optional

To make the cake, preheat the oven to 350 degrees F. Grease three 8-inch round cake pans.

Place the butter in a large mixing bowl and beat with a hand mixer on high speed until creamy. Beat in the sugar until combined. Add the egg yolks, one at a time, beating well after each addition. Add the vanilla and fruit spread.

Sift the flour and baking soda into a medium bowl.

Alternately add the flour mixture and buttermilk to the egg mixture, beating on medium speed until just incorporated. Fold in the diced strawberries.

Clean the beaters and dry completely. Place the egg whites in a medium bowl and beat until stiff peaks form. Gently fold the beaten egg whites into the batter.

Divide the batter among the cake pans. Bake for 25 to 28 minutes, until a wooden pick inserted near the center comes out clean. Let stand for 10 minutes in the pans, then remove from the pans and place on a wire rack to cool completely. Refrigerate the cakes until ready to use.

To make the icing, place the butter in a large mixing bowl and beat with a hand mixer on high speed until creamy. Gradually add the powdered sugar and strawberries, mixing after each addition until combined. Fold in the pecans and coconut.

To assemble, place one cake layer on a cake stand or plate. Spread a generous amount of icing on top of the cake. Place a second cake layer on top of the icing, and spread another generous amount of icing on the top. Place the third cake layer on top of the icing, and spread and swirl the remaining icing on the top layer of cake. Do not ice the sides. Refrigerate until ready to serve.

◗ *Makes 10 to 12 servings.*

Note: Make sure you sift and then measure the all-purpose flour in this recipe.

Chocolate-Hazelnut Spread Banana Cobbler

Cobbler is one of those nostalgic Southern desserts I remember learning to make early on in the kitchen with my mom. Cobbler is normally created as a celebration of the ripening fruits of summer, but this particular cobbler has a decadent twist. Bubbling butter, brown sugar, and banana slices caramelize until golden before the cobbler batter is poured over the top and dotted with frozen chunks of chocolate-hazelnut spread and placed in the oven to bake. The result: a fudgy, caramelized banana center with a sweet and crunchy exterior—a comforting ending to any meal.

3/4 cup plus 1 tablespoon chocolate-hazelnut spread

4 tablespoons butter, divided

1/4 cup plus 2 tablespoons firmly packed light brown sugar

2 small ripe bananas, sliced diagonally about 3/8 inch thick

1 cup self-rising flour

1/2 cup pure cane sugar

1 cup whole milk

1 teaspoon pure vanilla extract

Homemade Whipped Cream (see recipe on page 293)

Spoon about 1 1/2 tablespoons of the chocolate-hazelnut spread in each section of an ice cube tray. Freeze for 2 to 4 hours or until firm.

Preheat the oven to 350 degrees F.

Melt 1 tablespoon of the butter in a 9-inch cast-iron skillet over medium heat. Sprinkle 2 tablespoons of the brown sugar evenly in the skillet. When the sugar has melted, add the banana slices in a single layer. Cook for 1 minute. Cut the remaining 3 tablespoons butter into cubes and add to the pan.

In a bowl mix together the flour, sugar, remaining 1/4 cup brown sugar, milk, and vanilla until combined. Remove the skillet from the heat and pour the milk mixture over the banana slices.

Remove the hazelnut cubes from the ice cube tray. Cut them into halves. Evenly distribute the pieces over the batter. Bake for 30 minutes. Let cool for 5 minutes.

Serve the cobbler warm with the Homemade Whipped Cream.

● *Makes 5 servings.*

Note: I prefer to use Nutella brand chocolate-hazelnut spread.

A Little "Nutty" Banana Pudding

|||||||||||||||||||||||||||||||||||||||||||||||||||||||||||||||||||||||||||||||||||||||||||||||||||||||||||||||||||||||||||||||||||||||||||||||||||||||||

My mom has always gone bananas over what she calls *real* banana pudding. Our family even planned trips around a stop at The Round Table in Mendenhall, Mississippi, for lunch and this dessert. The Round Table has been around since the early 1900s and was known for its revolving tables and family-style service. With a spin of the table center, every kind of Sunday "come to dinner" dish magically appears in front of you, including desserts that do not disappoint, especially old-fashioned banana pudding. With each bite, layers of flavor hit your tongue. First, the soft marshmallowy meringue. Second, the rich vanilla custard. And finally, the natural sweet and creamy banana and the wafers that form the cake crust. It's a real banana pudding, just like my grandma made and my mom still makes. This recipe is my twist on the classic. I wanted to reduce the amount of sugar, so I've replaced some of it with an easy-to-make pistachio powder. It's still rich, creamy, and delicious, a real Southern comfort dessert that just went a little nutty.

2 tablespoons raw shelled pistachios

1/3 cup plus 4 tablespoons pure cane sugar, divided

1/3 cup all-purpose flour

Dash of salt

3 large eggs, separated

2 1/4 cups skim milk

1/2 teaspoon pure vanilla extract

32 vanilla wafers

5 ripe bananas, sliced

Preheat the oven to 350 degrees F.

Place the pistachios in a spice grinder and process until a powder forms to equal 2 tablespoons pistachio powder.

Combine 1/3 cup of the sugar, pistachio powder, flour, and salt in the top of a double boiler. In a bowl whisk together the egg yolks and milk. Whisk the egg mixture into the flour mixture. Add water to the bottom of the double boiler. Do not allow the water to touch the bottom of the top pan. Cook over slightly boiling water, stirring constantly, until the pudding thickens and coats the back of a spoon, 8 to 10 minutes. Remove the pan from the heat and stir in the vanilla.

Place a single layer of vanilla wafers in the bottom of an 8-inch square glass baking dish or in multiple mason jars. Add a single layer of banana slices over the wafers. Spoon half of the pudding over the bananas and spread evenly. Repeat layers of wafers, bananas, and pudding.

In a deep, medium bowl, beat the egg whites using a hand mixer on high speed until soft peaks form. Reduce the speed to low and gradually add the remaining 4 tablespoons sugar until incorporated. Increase the speed to high and beat until stiff peaks form. Spread the meringue on top of the pudding layer in the baking dish or mason jars. Using the back of a spoon, create peaks in the meringue.

Bake the banana pudding for 20 minutes or until the meringue is lightly brown. If using mason jars, place the jars on a baking sheet and bake for 8 to 10 minutes. Let stand for a few minutes before serving warm, or serve at room temperature.

○ *Makes 10 to 12 servings.*

Toasted Coconut Cream Pie with Chocolate and Pecans

My sister Brittyn's all-time favorite dessert is coconut cream pie. My mom and I teamed up in the kitchen this year to create a special birthday pie for her. Our version is a combination of a creamy pie and a magic cookie bar (our favorite dessert bar).

1 graham cracker piecrust
1 cup plus 2 tablespoons sweetened
    shredded coconut, divided
1 (13 1/2-ounce) can unsweetened
    coconut milk
1 cup whole milk
1 cup pure cane sugar, divided
2 tablespoons all-purpose flour

2 tablespoons cornstarch
1/8 teaspoon fine sea salt
4 large eggs
1 tablespoon unsalted butter
1 tablespoon coconut cream, optional
2 tablespoons chopped pecans
1/2 ounce semisweet chocolate bar

Preheat the oven to 375 degrees F.

Bake the piecrust for 6 minutes or until golden brown. Set aside to cool.

Spread 1/2 cup of the shredded coconut on a baking sheet. Bake for 5 minutes, stirring halfway through the baking time. Let cool.

Combine the coconut milk, milk, and 3/4 cup of the sugar in a saucepan. Whisk in the flour and cornstarch until smooth. Heat over medium to medium-high heat until hot, about 5 minutes.

Remove the pan from the heat. Stir in the salt.

Separate the egg yolks from the whites into 2 medium bowls. Whisk the egg yolks, and temper them by whisking a small amount of the hot milk mixture into the egg yolks and then whisking the egg yolk mixture into the saucepan. Return the pan to the heat and cook until the mixture thickens and coats the back of a spoon, about 12 minutes. Remove the pan from the heat and stir in the toasted coconut, 1/2 cup of the untoasted coconut, and butter. To intensify the coconut flavor, stir in the coconut cream. Pour the filling into the prepared crust and let cool completely.

Beat the egg whites with a hand mixer on high speed until soft peaks form. Reduce the speed to low and gradually add the remaining 1/4 cup sugar. Increase the speed to high and beat until stiff peaks form. Spread the meringue over the top of the pie, creating peaks with the back of a spoon.

Sprinkle the remaining 2 tablespoons untoasted coconut and chopped pecans on top. Bake until the meringue is golden brown, about 6 minutes. Use a vegetable peeler to shave the length of the chocolate bar on top of the toasted meringue. Serve immediately or refrigerate until ready to serve.

◗ *Makes 6 to 8 servings.*

Oatmeal Lace Cookies

My favorite cookie combination is crunchy and chewy. I was inspired to create this recipe after having a crunchy and chewy flourless oatmeal cookie at a cheese shop in La Jolla, California. It was one of the best cookies I have ever tasted. On the day I was craving those memorable cookies, I only had maple and brown sugar instant oatmeal packets, so I created my Oatmeal Lace Cookies, with their delicate lace-like edges, using these instant packet ingredients.

1/3 cup butter

3 packets maple and brown sugar
   instant oatmeal

1/3 cup pure cane sugar

1/3 cup firmly packed light brown sugar

1/8 teaspoon fine salt

1 teaspoon pure vanilla extract

1 large egg

Almond slices for garnish, optional

Melted dark chocolate for garnish,
   optional

Melt the butter in a medium microwave-safe bowl. Add the oatmeal, cane sugar, brown sugar, and salt. Stir the mixture together. Stir in the vanilla and egg until combined.

Cover the bowl with plastic wrap and refrigerate for 20 minutes.

Preheat the oven to 350 degrees F. Line a baking sheet with a silicon mat or parchment paper.

Using a small ice cream scooper, drop mounds of the chilled dough 2 to 3 inches apart on the lined baking sheet. Flatten slightly. (Make sure there's enough room for each cookie to spread.)

Bake the cookies for 10 to 12 minutes, until the edges have browned. The cookies will continue to cook on the baking sheet. Allow the cookies to cool on the pan for about 5 minutes before using an offset spatula to gently transfer them to a wire rack to cool completely and harden.

Garnish with the almonds and a drizzle of the chocolate.

◐ *Makes about 1 1/2 dozen cookies.*

Notes: Use Oatmeal Lace Cookies to make cannoli. Wrap the warm cookies around the greased handle of a wooden spoon, and gently press together to form a cylinder. Allow the cannoli cookies to cool completely before removing from the spoon handle. To serve, pipe a sweetened ricotta cheese into the center of the cookies.

You also can make dessert bowls from Oatmeal Lace Cookies. Turn a muffin pan upside down and grease the outer cups. Place the warm cookies over the cups and lightly press to shape. Let cool completely before removing. To serve, scoop ice cream into the cooled dessert bowls.

Southern Candy Bar

||||||||||||||||||||||||||||||||||||||||||||||||||||||||||||||||||||||||||||||||||||||||||||||||||||||||||||||||||||||||||||||||||||

For my first cookbook I created a crispy coconut bites recipe that featured pantry staples, including grits, and here I've changed the recipe into a candy bar. Grits for dessert? Yes, this candy bar will blow your mind. I've combined quick-cooking grits with coconut water and coconut milk to achieve an intense coconut flavor. I've also added shredded coconut to mimic the texture of the grits. This is a perfect treat to make and share with your "un-Southern" friends, especially if they have never experienced grits.

1 cup coconut water

1/3 cup coconut milk

1/2 cup quick-cooking grits

2 tablespoons pure cane sugar

1/2 cup sweetened shredded coconut

1/2 pound milk, semisweet, or dark chocolate bar

12 pecan halves, toasted

Line an 8½ x 4½-inch glass loaf pan with waxed paper, allowing a 2-inch overhang on all sides.

Mix together the coconut water and milk in a saucepan and bring to a low boil over medium-high heat. Whisk in the grits and reduce the heat to low. Cook, stirring occasionally, until the grits reach porridge consistency, about 5 minutes. Remove the pan from the heat and stir in the sugar and coconut.

Spoon the grits mixture into the loaf pan. Spread evenly with a rubber spatula and let cool at room temperature for 2 hours or until slightly firm.

After 2 hours, carefully remove the coconut mixture from the pan by pulling the sides of the waxed paper. Place the loaf on a cutting board and cut it into 12 rectangles.

Fill the bottom of a double boiler with a few inches of water. Bring the water to a simmer over medium heat. Chop the chocolate into small chunks and place one-third in the top of the double boiler. Once the chocolate begins to melt, stir it. Add the remaining chocolate chunks in two batches, stirring until melted and smooth after each addition. Carefully remove the bowl from the heat and transfer to the counter.

Lay a large piece of waxed paper on the counter. Place one of the grits bars on a slotted spatula, and place a pecan half in the middle of the bar. Holding the spatula over the bowl of chocolate, spoon the melted chocolate over the bar until completely coated. Lightly tap the spatula against the bowl to remove the excess chocolate. To cover the bottom of the bar, spoon a line the size of the grits bar onto the waxed paper. Using a butter knife, slide the grits bar onto the line of chocolate. Repeat with the rest of the grits bars. Let cool until the chocolate has hardened.

Enjoy immediately or store in an airtight container.

○ *Makes 12 bars.*

Blueberry-Pecan Crunch

In June when blueberries are in abundance, Mrs. Dutchie, an elderly family friend, would make her blueberry crunch for my family. She would greet us at the door of her home with her blueberry dessert after we had all spent the day at Poplarville's blueberry jubilee. One bite and we were in a happy sugar coma. On the eve of the blueberry jubilee this year, I created a version of her dessert as a way for my family to remember the sweet hospitality of Mrs. Dutchie. My version includes less sugar and butter and features a crunchy butter pecan crust.

1 (20-ounce) can crushed pineapple in 100 percent pineapple juice

3 cups fresh blueberries

2/3 cup pure cane sugar

1 (15.25-ounce) box butter pecan cake mix

3/4 cup (1 1/4 sticks) butter

1 cup chopped pecans

1/8 teaspoon coarse sea salt

Homemade Whipped Cream (see recipe on page 293) or vanilla ice cream, for serving

Preheat the oven to 350 degrees F.

Pour the crushed pineapple in the bottom of a 12-inch cast-iron skillet or a 9 x 13-inch glass baking dish. Evenly distribute the blueberries over the top. Sprinkle the sugar and then the cake mix over the blueberries.

Melt the butter in a microwave-safe bowl and pour it over the top of the cake mix. Be sure to cover it all. Sprinkle the chopped pecans and coarse salt on top. Bake the cake for 50 minutes or until golden brown. Serve warm with Homemade Whipped Cream or vanilla ice cream.

● *Makes 6 to 8 servings.*

White Hot Chocolate

One of my family's earliest Christmas traditions was movie night. During the nights preceding Christmas, we gather to watch our collection of Christmas movies, ranging from *Home Alone* to *The Grinch*. And Christmas movie night means special snacks, such as my homemade caramel popcorn, and an assortment of warm drinks. This White Hot Chocolate is a new addition to our old family tradition, and I have a feeling it will soon find a place in your family traditions as well.

4 cups whole milk

1 cup heavy cream

4 ounces white chocolate, chopped

Homemade Whipped Cream (see recipe on page 293) for serving, optional

Shaved white chocolate for garnish

Combine the milk and cream in a medium saucepan. Cook over medium heat until warm.

Add the chopped white chocolate to a medium bowl. Pour the warm milk and cream over the chocolate. Let stand for 2 minutes, then whisk until combined and smooth. Serve warm in mugs topped with Homemade Whipped Cream and shaved white chocolate.

◗ *Makes 4 servings.*

Variations

For a lavender-lemon white hot chocolate, add 4 teaspoons dried culinary lavender and 1/4 teaspoon finely grated lemon zest to the milk mixture. Cook for 5 minutes. Strain over the bowl of white chocolate. Whisk to combine, and serve.

For a cookies-and-cream white hot chocolate, remove and discard the cream filling from 8 chocolate sandwich cookies. Add the cookies to the white hot chocolate. Let soften for 2 minutes, then whisk until combined and smooth. Serve topped with Homemade Whipped Cream and chocolate cookie pieces.

Cracker Jack Panna Cotta

My mom's go-to restaurant desserts are creamy ones, including crème brulée, flan, and panna cotta. I, on the other hand, like textured desserts. To please both palates, I created a creamy and crunchy dessert with my Cracker Jack Panna Cotta featuring a smooth buttery-popcorn-flavored panna cotta and crunchy toasted peanut and popcorn topping with caramel drizzled over the top.

1 cup half-and-half, divided

1 cup whole milk

1 1/2 cups popped butter-flavored popcorn, divided

1 1/2 teaspoons unflavored gelatin powder

1/4 cup pure cane sugar

Homemade Caramel (see recipe on page 292)

1 1/4 teaspoons flaky sea salt

2 tablespoons shelled and skinned peanuts

Grease four 3-inch ramekins or 4 cups of a muffin pan.

Mix together ¾ cup of the half-and-half and milk in a heavy medium saucepan, and heat over medium heat. Add 1 cup popcorn and cook for 8 minutes to infuse the mixture with popcorn flavor.

Meanwhile, pour the remaining ¼ cup half-and-half into a shallow bowl. Sprinkle the gelatin over the half-and-half and let stand for 10 minutes.

Strain the popcorn-milk mixture through a fine mesh strainer into a bowl, and discard the popcorn. Return the milk to the saucepan and add the sugar, whisking to dissolve. Remove from the heat and stir in the softened gelatin mixture, whisking until it dissolves. If any gelatin particles remain, stir over low heat until they dissolve.

Strain the milk mixture through a fine mesh strainer into a large measuring bowl or container for easy pouring. Fill the ramekins or cups. Cover with plastic wrap and refrigerate until set, 2 to 4 hours.

Combine the Homemade Caramel and flaky sea salt in a bowl.

Toast the peanuts in a small sauté pan over medium heat for 2 to 3 minutes, stirring occasionally. Transfer the peanuts to a cutting board and chop into small pieces.

To assemble, gently run a butter knife around the sides of the panna cottas and unmold onto small dessert plates. Top each panna cotta with some of the remaining ½ cup popcorn and the peanuts. Drizzle about 1 tablespoon of the salted caramel on top and serve immediately.

● *Makes 4 servings.*

Buttermilk Pecan Pralines

When people tell me they are visiting New Orleans for the first time, I tell them they can't go home before sampling some piping hot beignets and pralines. During one trip with my family, my dad took his praline love to a new level. After having Sunday brunch at the Royal Sonesta, I noticed his pockets were full. When I asked why, he pulled out a napkin that was full of pralines. All-you-can-eat to him included their pralines. We still laugh about his obsession every time I make these Buttermilk Pecan Pralines. If you can't make it to New Orleans, this sweet treat will satisfy your longing.

1 cup pure cane sugar
1 cup firmly packed light brown sugar
3/4 cup buttermilk
2 tablespoons butter

1/8 teaspoon salt
2 cups pecan halves
3/4 teaspoon pure vanilla extract
3/4 teaspoon baking soda

Liberally grease a large piece of waxed paper.

In a large heavy saucepan, combine the cane sugar, brown sugar, buttermilk, butter, and salt. Cook over medium-low heat, stirring constantly with a wooden spoon, until the sugars dissolve. Stir in the pecans. Cover and cook over medium heat for 3 minutes. Remove the lid and with a wet pastry brush, wipe down the sides of the saucepan to remove any sugar crystals.

Cook until the mixture reaches the soft-ball stage, about 235 degrees F, stirring constantly.

Remove the pan from the heat and stir in the vanilla and baking soda. Beat the mixture with the wooden spoon until it thickens and the bubbles subside.

Immediately drop the praline mixture by tablespoonfuls onto the waxed paper. Let cool completely and harden, about 15 minutes.

Makes about 2 dozen pralines.

Note: Do not make these on a rainy or highly humid day or the pralines will not set up.

Hello Dolly Ice Cream Sandwiches

Hello Dolly Ice Cream Sandwiches are a cool, delicious, and decidedly different dessert for spring get-togethers, whether they're casual barbecues or garden club luncheons. The rich, spiced cookies and the toasted coconut and nuts add layers of flavor and contrasting textures to this out-of-the-ordinary ice cream sandwich. For a fun, interactive party, set up an ice cream sandwich station with a variety of toppings to allow guests to customize their own.

1/2 cup butter

3/4 cup cookie spread, such as Biscoff European Cookie Spread

1/4 cup molasses

1/4 cup pure cane sugar

1/4 cup firmly packed light brown sugar

1 large egg

1 1/2 cups all-purpose flour

1/2 cup graham cracker crumbs

2 teaspoons baking soda

1/2 teaspoon fine sea salt

3/4 cup dark chocolate chips

3/4 cup chopped pecans

1 2/3 cups sweetened shredded coconut

1/2 gallon Creole cream cheese ice cream, slightly softened

Preheat the oven to 375 degrees F. Line a baking sheet with a silicone mat or parchment paper.

Melt the butter in a medium microwave-safe bowl. Let cool slightly. Add the cookie spread, molasses, cane sugar, brown sugar, and egg. Whisk until combined.

In a small bowl whisk together the flour, graham cracker crumbs, baking soda, and salt. Add to the butter mixture, stirring until just combined.

Using a small ice cream scoop, drop the dough in mounds 2 inches apart on the lined baking sheet. Gently press each mound with the bottom of a greased glass to about 1/4 inch thick.

Bake for 5 minutes. Let cool on the pan for 3 minutes, then transfer to a wire rack to cool completely.

Melt the dark chocolate chips in a small microwave-safe bowl in 45-second increments until the chocolate begins to melt, stirring gently after each heating. Spread a thin layer of the melted chocolate over the bottom of each cooled cookie. Set aside to harden.

Spread the chopped pecans on one end of a baking sheet and the coconut on the other end. Bake for 4 minutes or until toasted and golden brown. Let cool.

To assemble the ice cream sandwiches, spoon about 1/4 cup of the ice cream onto the chocolate-coated side of one cookie, and top with a second cookie, chocolate side facing the ice cream.

Roll one side of the exposed ice cream in the toasted pecans and the other side in the toasted coconut. Repeat the process, using the remaining cookies, coconut, and pecans.

Serve immediately or place on a baking sheet and freeze until ready to serve.

● *Makes 15 ice cream sandwiches.*

Note: Creole cream cheese ice cream is a Southern regional ice cream flavor. If you cannot find it in the freezer section of your grocery store, use a tart frozen yogurt or vanilla ice cream.

Mini Lemon Meringue Pies

||||||||||||||||||||||||||||||||||||||||||||||||||||||||||||||||||||||||||||||||||||||||||||||||||||||||||||||||||||||||||||||||||||||||||||||

Sunday lunch at my great-grandmother Strahan's house often ended with a slice of her famous lemon meringue pie. She used lemons from the tree in her backyard. She picked them when they were ripe and stored them in the freezer so she could make her famous pie all year long. This is my bite-size version of her pies. They make the perfect party treat.

1 cup pure cane sugar, divided
2 tablespoons all-purpose flour
2 tablespoons cornstarch
Pinch of fine sea salt
3/4 cup hot water

3 eggs, separated
1/2 cup fresh lemon juice
1/8 teaspoon finely grated lemon zest
1 recipe Olive Oil Pie Dough (see recipe on page 291)

In a medium saucepan mix together 3/4 cup of the sugar, flour, cornstarch, and salt. Gradually stir in the hot water until combined. Bring to a boil over medium-high heat, stirring constantly until the sugar dissolves. Remove the pan from the heat.

In a medium bowl whisk the egg yolks. Whisk a small amount of the hot sugar mixture into the egg yolks, and then whisk the tempered egg mixture into the saucepan. Return the pan to the heat, and cook for 1 minute on medium heat. Whisk in the lemon juice and zest. Reduce the heat to medium-low and cook until the mixture thickens and coats the back of a spoon, about 5 minutes, whisking constantly. Let cool completely.

Preheat the oven to 350 F. Grease two 24-cup mini muffin pans.

Roll out half of the Olive Oil Pie Dough to a round about 1/8 inch thick. Using a 2 3/4-inch fluted cookie cutter, cut the dough into rounds. Lightly press each round with your fingers until it is a little thinner. Place each round in a muffin cup, using your fingertips to press the dough into the bottom and up the sides of the cup. Repeat with the remaining half of the dough. Use a toothpick to prick holes in the bottom and sides of the dough. Bake for about 16 minutes, until lightly golden brown. Transfer the mini crusts to a wire rack to cool completely.

Place the mini pie shells on a baking sheet and spoon about 1 tablespoon of the lemon filling into each.

Beat the egg whites using a hand mixer on high speed until soft peaks form. Reduce the speed to low and gradually add the remaining 1/4 cup sugar. Increase the speed to high and beat until almost stiff peaks are formed. Spoon the meringue over each filled pie. Bake for about 5 minutes, until the meringue peaks are golden brown. Let cool completely and serve.

◗ *Makes 33 mini pies and about 2 cups of filling.*

Note: The mini piecrusts and lemon filling can be made ahead for easy assembly.

Mississippi Mud Pie

A friend visiting Hattiesburg, Mississippi, asked where she could experience the famous Mississippi Mud Pie, but I didn't have an answer for her. There wasn't a restaurant in Hattiesburg that served it. So when a chef friend at Vicki's on Walnut asked me to create the dessert menu for the restaurant, I knew which dessert to feature first. This Mississippi Mud Pie's fudgy center and crackle topping are a result of the Brownie Cookie batter filling. A slightly tart cream cheese topping takes this pie over the top.

12 tablespoons butter

3 1/2 cups graham cracker crumbs

Brownie Cookie batter, unchilled (see recipe on page 270)

4 ounces cream cheese, softened

1 cup heavy cream

4 tablespoons powdered sugar

1 cup pecan halves, chopped

1/2 teaspoon fine sea salt

Chocolate shavings for garnish

Preheat the oven to 350 degrees F. Grease two 9-inch tart pans with removable bottoms.

Melt the butter in a microwave-safe bowl. Add the graham cracker crumbs and mix until the crumbs are evenly moistened. Divide the mixture between the tart pans. Press into the bottom and up the sides of the tart pans. Place on a baking sheet and bake for 5 minutes. The crust should be set and slightly firm to the touch. Transfer the tart pans to a wire rack to cool slightly.

Divide the Brownie Cookie batter between the prepared crusts. With the back of a spoon, smooth the top of the batter. Bake for 25 to 30 minutes, until the crust is golden brown and the filling is set. The pies will be fudgy. Transfer to a wire rack to cool for about 10 minutes.

While the tart is cooling, place the cream cheese in a medium bowl. Using an electric mixer on high speed, beat the cream cheese until smooth. Add the heavy cream and beat until soft peaks form. Gradually add the powdered sugar, beating until combined. Continue beating on medium speed until thickened.

Heat a medium sauté pan over medium heat. Add the pecan pieces and salt. Cook the pecans until toasted, about 2 minutes, tossing occasionally. Let cool.

Remove the warm tarts from the pans, and place on serving plates. Slice into wedges and top with the whipped cream mixture, salted pecan pieces, and chocolate shavings.

● *Makes 2 tarts.*

Gluten-Free Bread Pudding

I had the honor of cooking a three-course menu at the 2013 ChefDance during the Sundance Film Festival. I needed to offer a gluten-free dessert option for my bread pudding, which at first seemed to be an impossible task. Through experimenting with ingredients, I discovered that substituting parsnips in place of the bread created a smooth, creamy, bread-like texture that had me going back for bite after bite.

Gluten-Free Bread Puddings

5 cups finely chopped parsnips (about 20 ounces)

1/2 cup (1 stick) butter

1 cup pure cane sugar

3 tablespoons brown rice flour

1 teaspoon baking powder

2 large eggs, beaten

1 teaspoon pure vanilla extract

Coconut-Maple Sauce

1 (13 1/2- ounce) can unsweetened coconut milk, refrigerated for 2 hours

3 teaspoons pure maple syrup

To make the Gluten-Free Bread Puddings, preheat the oven to 350 degrees F. Grease 8 (8-ounce) ramekins.

Place the parsnips in a medium saucepan and cover with water. Bring the water to a boil over medium-high heat. Cook until the parsnips are fork tender. Drain and place half of the parsnips in a ricer* to press the water out of them. Transfer the strained parsnips to the bowl of a food processor. Puree until smooth. Transfer the puree to a bowl and repeat with the remaining parsnips.

Melt the butter in a large microwave-safe bowl. Add the parsnip puree, sugar, rice flour, baking powder, eggs, and vanilla. Mix until well blended. Divide the mixture evenly among the ramekins. Place the ramekins in a 9 x 13-inch glass baking dish. Fill the baking dish with water to just above halfway up the ramekins. Cover the baking dish with a sheet of parchment paper and bake for 25 minutes. Remove the ramekins from the water bath and let stand for 5 minutes. Run a butter knife around the edge of each ramekin and invert the puddings onto a plate. Serve warm with the Coconut-Maple Sauce.

To make the Coconut-Maple Sauce, remove the thick creamy white layer off the top of the cold coconut milk in the can and place in a small bowl. It should measure about 1/2 cup. Use the remaining coconut milk in a smoothie, if desired. Whisk in the maple syrup until combined. Gently warm the sauce in a small saucepan over low heat. Serve warm over the puddings.

◉ *Makes 8 servings.*

*If you don't have a ricer, press the parsnips through a wire mesh strainer using a rubber spatula.

Old-Fashioned Fudge Popsicles

Several summers ago, I was all about popsicles. It began as a fund-raising effort for the Myasthenia Gravis foundation, a charity near and dear to my heart because of my dad's condition. A popsicle maker company generously donated several freezable popsicle makers for me to use to develop lots of recipes for frozen treats on a stick. Out of all of the icy and creamy selections, everyone's favorite turned out to be my Old-Fashioned Fudge Popsicle. Like the original, it has a deep, rich, chocolaty flavor, but less sugar and fat than the store-bought version.

1/4 cup chopped semisweet chocolate

1/4 cup plus 1 tablespoon light agave syrup

3 tablespoons unsweetened cocoa powder

2 tablespoons cornstarch

2 cups whole or 2 percent reduced-fat milk

1 1/2 teaspoons pure vanilla extract

Pinch of fine sea salt

Melt the chopped chocolate in a medium saucepan over medium-low heat, stirring occasionally. Stir in the agave, cocoa powder, cornstarch, and milk. Increase the heat to medium and cook, whisking constantly, until the mixture thickens, about 10 minutes. Stir in the vanilla and salt. Transfer the chocolate mixture to a bowl and let cool to room temperature.

Pour the cooled popsicle mixture into eight 1/3-cup popsicle molds, then insert a wooden stick into each mold. Freeze until firm.

Run hot water over the molds to loosen the popsicles before unmolding.

● *Makes 8 servings.*

Caramelized Banana Butter Pecan Cake with Oat-Pecan Crumble

||||||||||||||||||||||||||||||||||||||||||||||||||||||||||||||||||||||||||||||||||||||||||||||||||||||||||||||||||||||||||

The abundance of nut trees growing on my family's land has always provided a source of food and fun for our family. I have many fond memories of collecting and roasting pecans for holiday meals. This cake gets its flavor from butter- and pecan-infused milk.

Butter Pecan Cake
|||||||||||||||||||||||||||||||||||||||||||||

Cooking spray

Flour for dusting pans

1/2 cup (1 stick) plus 1 tablespoon
    butter, softened, divided

1/2 cup pecan halves

1/2 cup whole milk

1 1/2 cups cake flour

1/2 teaspoon baking powder

1/2 teaspoon baking soda

1/4 teaspoon fine sea salt

1/2 cup firmly packed light brown sugar

1/2 cup pure cane sugar

2 large eggs, room temperature

1 teaspoon pure vanilla extract

1/4 cup buttermilk, room temperature

1/4 cup Homemade Caramel (see recipe
    on page 292)

Caramelized Bananas
||||||||||||||||||||||||||||||||||||||||||||||

2 medium ripe bananas

1 tablespoon butter, divided

3 tablespoons firmly packed light
    brown sugar, divided

Oat-Pecan Crumble
||||||||||||||||||||||||||||||||||||||||||||||

2 tablespoons butter

1 cup old-fashioned oats

3 tablespoons chopped pecans

1/4 teaspoon ground cinnamon

1/8 teaspoon fine sea salt

3 tablespoons firmly packed light
    brown sugar

1 tablespoon honey

1 tablespoon maple syrup

Yogurt Whipped Cream
||||||||||||||||||||||||||||||||||||||||||||||

3/4 cup heavy cream

1/4 cup plain Greek yogurt

3 tablespoons powdered sugar

To make the cake, preheat the oven to 350 degrees F. Grease two 8-inch round cake pans with cooking spray. Lightly dust with flour.

    Melt 1 tablespoon of the butter in a small saucepan over medium heat. Add the pecans and cook for 5 minutes, stirring occasionally. Add the milk and reduce the heat to low. Cover and cook for 20 minutes. Place a wire mesh strainer over a small bowl and strain the milk. Discard the pecans. Let cool slightly.

In a medium bowl, sift the flour, baking powder, baking soda, and salt.

Place the remaining 1/2 cup butter in a large bowl. Using an electric mixer on medium speed, beat until soft and creamy. Gradually add the brown sugar and cane sugar, and beat until well blended. Add the eggs one at a time, beating after each addition. Add the vanilla and beat until blended.

Add the buttermilk to the cooled pecan milk.

Alternately add the flour mixture and milk mixture to the batter, beginning and ending with the flour mixture and beating well after each addition.

Divide the batter evenly between the two pans. Smooth the tops with an offset spatula. Bake for 20 to 22 minutes, until a wooden pick inserted near the center comes out clean. Place the cakes on a wire rack to cool for about 10 minutes. Invert the cakes onto the rack to cool completely.

Reduce the oven temperature to 325 degrees F.

While the cakes are cooling, make the Caramelized Bananas. Cut the bananas on a diagonal into 1/4-inch-thick slices. Place a sheet of waxed paper in a small baking pan and set aside.

Melt 1/2 tablespoon of the butter in a 9-inch cast-iron skillet over medium heat. Sprinkle 1 1/2 tablespoons of the brown sugar evenly in the skillet. Cook until the sugar begins to melt. Increase the heat to medium-high if necessary. Add the slices from one banana. Cook for about 1 minute, until the bottoms of the banana slices are caramelized. Flip and cook for another 30 seconds. Transfer to the waxed paper. Wipe the skillet clean and repeat the process with the remaining ingredients.

To make the Oat-Pecan Crumble, melt the butter in a medium microwave-safe bowl. Add the oats, pecans, cinnamon, salt, sugar, honey, and maple syrup. Stir together and transfer to a baking sheet. Bake for 10 minutes at 325 degrees F. Toss the granola with a spoon. Bake for another 12 minutes. Toss the granola and let cool.

To assemble the cake, transfer one of the cake layers to a 9-inch cast-iron skillet, and evenly cover with half of the Caramelized Bananas. Drizzle 1 tablespoon of the Homemade Caramel over the bananas and cake. Place the second layer on top. Repeat with the remaining banana slices and another tablespoon caramel. Cover the pan with aluminum foil and bake for 15 minutes at 325 degrees F. Top the warm cake with the crumble and drizzle with additional caramel.

To make the Yogurt Whipped Cream, beat the cream in a medium bowl using an electric mixer on high speed until thickened. Add the yogurt and beat until soft peaks form. Gradually add the powdered sugar until combined.

Slice the cake into wedges and serve warm with the Yogurt Whipped Cream.

● *Makes 6 servings.*

Dark Chocolate Granola

I created this dessert in order to satisfy my craving for chocolate in a healthier way. Rich and decadent cocoa powder is paired with oats, pistachios, dark chocolate chips, and dried cranberries to create the perfect combination of sweet and tangy crunch. Enjoy for a satisfying dessert without the guilt.

1 tablespoon butter

1 tablespoon extra-virgin olive oil

3 to 4 tablespoons honey

1 teaspoon brewed coffee

2 tablespoons dark chocolate cocoa powder

1 cup old-fashioned rolled oats

Pinch of fine sea salt

2 tablespoons shelled and skinned unsalted pistachios

1 tablespoon sweetened dried cranberries

2 tablespoons dark chocolate chips

Preheat the oven to 325 degrees F.

Melt the butter in a medium microwave-safe bowl. Add the olive oil, honey, coffee, cocoa powder, oats, and salt. Pour onto a baking sheet and spread evenly with the back of a spoon. Bake for 10 minutes. Toss with a spoon. Bake for an additional 5 to 8 minutes. Remove from the oven, toss again, and let cool for 10 minutes. Add the pistachios, cranberries, and dark chocolate chips. Serve or store in an airtight container for up to 1 week.

◗ *Makes about 1 1/2 cups.*

Brownie Cookies

Sometimes a person will ask, "What is your favorite go-to dessert?" I have to admit, in my home I have occasionally made brownies several nights in a row. Of course, there is always the inevitable fight over who gets to lick the spoon and the last drops of batter in the bowl. My Brownie Cookies represent the best of what I like about brownies: crisp brownie edges and fudgy centers. I love to see the look of delight on someone's face when he or she bites into one and discovers the unexpected rich, fudgy center. Love at first, second, and third bite!

3 ounces unsweetened chocolate bar, chopped
14 ounces semisweet chocolate bar, chopped, divided
1/2 cup (1 stick) butter, softened
4 large eggs
1/4 cup chocolate-hazelnut spread

1 1/4 cups pure cane sugar
1 tablespoon brewed coffee
1/2 teaspoon pure vanilla extract
1/2 cup all-purpose flour
1/2 teaspoon baking powder
1/4 teaspoon fine sea salt

Preheat the oven to 350 degrees F. Line a baking sheet with parchment paper.

In a microwave-safe bowl combine the unsweetened chocolate, 11 ounces of the semisweet chocolate, and butter. Microwave in 1-minute increments until melted, stirring after each minute. Set aside to cool.

In a large bowl stir together the eggs, chocolate-hazelnut spread, sugar, coffee, and vanilla.

In a small bowl sift together the flour, baking powder, and salt.

Gradually add the melted chocolate mixture to the egg mixture. Stir to combine. Fold in the flour mixture until combined. Stir in the remaining 3 ounces chopped semisweet chocolate and refrigerate the dough for up to 1 hour.

Scoop out heaping tablespoonsful of dough and roll in your hands to form 11 balls. Place on the prepared baking sheet and bake for 8 minutes or until the cookies are set but slightly fudgy. Let the cookies stand on the baking sheet for 1 minute before transferring to a wire rack to cool slightly. Repeat with the remaining dough. Serve warm.

◉ *Makes about 2 1/2 dozen cookies.*

Note: I prefer to use Nutella brand chocolate-hazelnut spread.

White Chocolate Bread Pudding Beignets

Whenever I go to New Orleans, just a short distance from my parents' home, I can't leave without a visit to Cafe Du Monde for an order of beignets and a glass of chocolate milk. The beignets' warm and crisp outer shell gives way to the soft, fluffy interior that is indescribably delicious. Since I can't always make a trip to New Orleans whenever I have a craving for beignets, I decided to take one of my other favorite desserts, bread pudding, and create a hybrid dessert that would combine the crunchy, fried goodness with a creamy white chocolate center. Make sure you keep a few for yourself before you share them with family and friends, because these small bites of goodness won't last long.

6 cups 1-inch French bread cubes, crusts removed

9 tablespoons half-and-half, divided

1/4 cup heavy cream

1 large egg

1 large egg yolk

2 tablespoons pure cane sugar

4 ounces white chocolate, chopped, divided

1/4 teaspoon pure vanilla extract

Vegetable or canola oil for frying

Powdered sugar for garnish

Preheat the oven to 350 degrees F.

Place the bread cubes on a baking sheet. Bake for 8 to 10 minutes, until golden brown. Place half of the bread cubes in a zip-top plastic bag. Crush into crumbs. Pour the crumbs into a wide, shallow bowl. Set the remaining bread cubes and the bread crumbs aside.

Place 5 tablespoons of the half-and-half and the heavy cream in a medium saucepan, and heat over medium heat. Bring to a simmer and cook for 7 minutes or until hot.

Meanwhile, whisk together the egg, egg yolk, and sugar in a large bowl. Slowly add the hot cream mixture, whisking constantly.

In the same saucepan melt 2 ounces of white chocolate with the remaining 4 tablespoons half-and-half over low heat, stirring occasionally. Gradually add to the egg mixture, whisking constantly. Stir in the vanilla. Lightly press the bread cubes into the white chocolate mixture to soak. Let soak for 5 minutes.

Line a baking sheet with waxed paper. Take 3 soaked bread cubes in your hand. Add a few pieces of the chopped white chocolate to the center. Form the bread around the chocolate and press together to form a ball. Roll in the bread crumbs and place on the lined baking sheet. Repeat with the rest of the soaked bread cubes and chocolate. Refrigerate for at least 2 hours.

Fill a large saucepan halfway with oil and heat to 350 degrees F. Line a baking sheet with paper towels. Fry the bread pudding balls for 3 minutes, turning halfway through the cooking time. Transfer to the paper towel–lined baking sheet to drain. Serve warm with a dusting of powdered sugar.

◗ *Makes 4 servings.*

Semi-Frozen Lime Pie with a Graham Brittle Crust

Before I visit a new place, I always do research to discover the local food favorites and famous foods of the area. While visiting Miami, my mom and I tried the famous Joe's Stone Crab and enjoyed not only the stone crabs but also the restaurant's semi-frozen key lime pie; it was cool and custardy. This lime pie is served semi-frozen too, but that's where the resemblance ends. Instead of the usual condensed milk, I folded whipped cream into the lime curd to create a creamy filling that rests on a unique candy-like crust of graham brittle. Try this new twist on an old classic the next time you want to show off.

Graham Brittle Crust

1/3 cup pure cane sugar

2 cups graham cracker crumbs

1/2 cup (1 stick) butter

Creamy Lime Filling

1 cup pure cane sugar

2 large eggs

2 large egg yolks

3/4 cup fresh lime juice

1/2 teaspoon finely grated lime zest

1/2 cup heavy cream

Homemade Whipped Cream (see recipe on page 293) for serving

To make the crust, preheat the oven to 350 degrees F. Grease a large tart pan or 5 small tart pans.

Spread the sugar in the bottom of a medium saucepan and cook over medium heat until sugar melts and turns an amber color, about 6 minutes.

Place the graham cracker crumbs in the bowl of a food processor. Melt the butter in a microwave-safe bowl, then add to the crumbs along with the sugar syrup. Process until combined.

Press the graham mixture into the bottom and up the sides of the pan(s). Bake for 10 minutes. Let cool.

To make the filling, mix together the sugar, eggs, egg yolks, and lime juice in a medium saucepan. Cook over medium heat until thickened, about 10 minutes, whisking constantly. Strain through a fine mesh strainer set over a medium bowl. Stir in the lime zest and refrigerate. The lime curd can be made a day ahead.

Pour the heavy cream into a medium bowl and beat with an electric mixer on high speed until soft peaks form. Fold into the chilled lime curd. Pour the creamy lime filling into the prepared graham brittle crust. Freeze for at least 2 hours or until set.

To serve, slice the semi-frozen pie into wedges and serve with the Homemade Whipped Cream.

◐ *Makes 1 large pie or 5 small pies.*

Essentials and Enhancers

As I develop recipes, there are some that become my go-to recipes for creating or enhancing other dishes. These are the ones you will see referenced in many other recipes in this book, and I recommend you keep the staple ingredients for these recipes in your pantry at all times.

Mint Pesto

Spinach Pesto

Pea Pesto

Mustard Green Pesto

Cornbread Crumbles

Spicy Pimento Cheese

Roasted Peanut Butter

Homemade Ketchup

Southern Verde Sauce

Roasted Grape Tomato Relish

Roasted Barbecue Sauce

Yogurt Aioli

Sriracha Spread

Roasted Garlic

Fried Sage Leaves

Olive Oil Pie Dough

Homemade Caramel

Homemade Whipped Cream

Mint Pesto

Mint Pesto pairs beautifully with Brie cheese as a topping for Dessert Toast (page 233).

1 tablespoon shelled and skinned pistachios

1/4 cup packed mint leaves (preferably apple mint)

4 teaspoons extra-virgin olive oil

Place the pistachios in the bowl of a food processor and process until a powder forms. Add the mint leaves and olive oil. Process the mixture until smooth, about 30 seconds. Use immediately.

▶ *Makes about 2 tablespoons.*

Spinach Pesto

I strive to grow a plentiful herb garden to supply all of my recipe testing needs, but some years my basil is far from plentiful. So when I'm creating a pesto, I often substitute easily accessible spinach leaves for expensive store-bought basil.

4 tablespoons chopped pecans

2 cloves garlic, sliced

8 cups firmly packed spinach leaves, stems removed

7 tablespoons extra-virgin olive oil

4 tablespoons grated Parmesan cheese

1/2 teaspoon fine sea salt

Toast the pecans in a medium skillet over medium-high heat until fragrant, tossing frequently. Transfer to a plate and let cool for 5 minutes.

Place the pecans and garlic in the bowl of a food processor and process until finely chopped. Add the spinach leaves, olive oil, cheese, and salt. Process until combined and almost smooth.

Use immediately or store in an airtight container in the refrigerator for up to 5 days.

▶ *Makes about 1 1/2 cups.*

Pea Pesto

Growing up, I remember our South Mississippi gardens typically contained the usual fresh field and/or black-eyed peas, but the only small green peas I remember came from cans. They were not very tasty. However, listening to my nanny Ida's tale of how much her dad loved fresh green peas from his North Mississippi garden, I was inspired to try them again. And wow! The difference in texture between canned peas and fresh ones may be eclipsed only by how much sweeter fresh ones taste. In this recipe I use frozen peas, which have a fresh taste and are accessible all year long. The creaminess of these little beauties lends itself perfectly to a pesto. I use it as the bottom layer for my Individual Southern Layered Salads (page 90), but it also makes an excellent replacement for mayonnaise on sandwiches. Once you taste it, I'm sure you'll think of other great uses for this versatile condiment.

2 cups frozen peas, thawed
2 tablespoons fresh chopped basil
2 teaspoons fresh chopped dill

1/2 teaspoon fine sea salt
1 tablespoon extra-virgin olive oil

Place the peas, basil, dill, salt, and oil in the bowl of a food processor and process until smooth. Use immediately or store in an airtight container in the refrigerator for up to 2 days.

◉ *Makes about 1 cup.*

Mustard Green Pesto

I love mustard greens and look for every opportunity to use them in a recipe. The soft leaves lend themselves well to a pesto. I serve it with my Crunchy Skillet Cornbread (page 121), but it also makes a flavorful spread for sandwiches, adds flavor to pasta dishes, and is a great base for my Shrimp Pesto Naan Pizza (page 166).

2 tablespoons chopped pecan halves
1 bunch fresh mustard greens
1 clove garlic, sliced
1 tablespoon butter

4 tablespoons extra-virgin olive oil
2 tablespoons grated Parmesan cheese
1/4 teaspoon fine sea salt

Toast the pecans in a medium skillet over medium-high heat until fragrant, tossing frequently. Transfer to a plate and let cool for 5 minutes.

Wash, drain, and pat dry the mustard greens. Cut off the stems and discard. Roughly chop the mustard greens. You should have about 4 cups.

Place the pecans and garlic in the bowl of a food processor and pulse until the mixture is finely chopped.

Melt the butter in a small microwave-safe bowl. Let cool for a few minutes and then add to the food processor. Add the mustard greens and olive oil and process until almost smooth. Add the cheese and salt. Pulse until combined. Season with additional salt to taste. Use immediately or store in an airtight container in the refrigerator for up to 5 days.

● *Makes 1 cup.*

Cornbread Crumbles

I use these Cornbread Crumbles to give crunch to foods that traditionally are fried (see "Fried" Green Tomatoes on page 142). I like to treat myself to fried food, but sometimes frying can be such a hassle, and I wanted to create healthier versions of some of my favorites that would be as crunchy as the oil-fried originals. After testing various toppings, I discovered that the toasted crumbs from my skillet cornbread had the perfect crunch.

1 pan Crunchy Skillet Cornbread (see recipe on page 121)

Preheat the oven to 400 degrees F.

Crumble the cornbread into small pieces over a baking sheet, and spread in an even layer. Bake for 22 minutes, until dry and crunchy, stirring halfway through the baking time. Let cool completely. Transfer the cooled crumbles to the bowl of a food processor. Pulse until almost fine crumbs form. Use immediately or store in an airtight container for up to 2 weeks.

◐ *Makes about 3 cups.*

Spicy Pimento Cheese

My first introduction to pimento cheese was the dainty pimento cheese-filled sandwiches served at church potlucks. I have to confess that I did not like it because of its sweet flavor. This version is spiced up with Sriracha.

2 ounces cream cheese, softened
1 1/2 tablespoons plain Greek yogurt
1 1/2 tablespoons mayonnaise
1 teaspoon Sriracha hot chili sauce
1 1/2 cups shredded sharp Cheddar cheese

1 1/2 cups shredded Colby Jack cheese
3/4 teaspoon cracked black pepper
Fine sea salt, to taste
1 tablespoon chopped pimientos

Combine the cream cheese, yogurt, mayonnaise, and chili sauce in a medium bowl until smooth. Add the Cheddar cheese, Colby Jack cheese, and pepper to the bowl. Stir to combine. Season the cheese mixture with salt to taste. Fold in the pimientos. Use immediately or store in the refrigerator for up to 1 week.

◐ *Makes 2 cups.*

Roasted Peanut Butter

Peanuts are plentiful in my home state of Mississippi. In season, you will find signs everywhere advertising boiled peanuts of all flavors, whether from a truck on the side of the road with a large pot or at a convenience store. I love peanut butter, but store-bought versions often have lots of sugar and sodium, so I started making my own. And so will you after you try this recipe.

2 cups shelled and skinned raw peanuts

Preheat the oven to 350 degrees F.

Place the peanuts on a baking sheet and roast for about 8 minutes. Transfer the nuts to the bowl of a food processor and process for 2 minutes. Scrape down the sides of the bowl and continue processing the nuts. The nuts will become a powder after about 5 minutes. Every few minutes, scrape down the sides of the food processor until the powder forms a paste. After 15 minutes, the peanut butter will be smooth. Store the peanut butter in a glass pint jar in the refrigerator for up to 2 weeks.

◗ *Makes about 2 cups.*

Note: You can use roasted unsalted peanuts and skip the roasting process, if you prefer.

Homemade Ketchup

When my dad was diagnosed with Myasthenia Gravis disease, he was prescribed a high-dose steroid. To help him reduce the potential side effects associated with this drug, I immediately began trying to reduce salt and sugar levels in his foods, including condiments. Not only is this ketchup healthier, it also tastes really good and is easy to make.

2 (8-ounce) cans no-salt-added tomato sauce

1/2 cup all-natural no-sugar-added apple juice

2 tablespoons sweetened dried cranberries

6 tablespoons honey

1 teaspoon apple cider vinegar

Combine the tomato sauce, apple juice, cranberries, honey, and vinegar in a small saucepan over medium heat. Cook for 10 minutes, stirring occasionally. Transfer the mixture to the bowl of a food processor and process until smooth. Return the mixture to the saucepan and cook over medium-low heat for an additional 10 minutes. Let cool and then refrigerate for up to 1 week.

◗ *Makes 2/3 cup.*

Southern Verde Sauce

My favorite Mexican sauce has always been a verde sauce. Since tomatillos are not always available where I live, I created my own version of the sauce using local green tomatoes. You'll find this sauce makes an appearance in the Pulled Pork Nachos (page 66) and Southern Carnitas (page 156), but it's also delicious on my Egg-in-a-Tortilla (page 30).

1/2 yellow onion, sliced
3 cloves garlic, sliced
3 medium green tomatoes, sliced
1/4 teaspoon fine sea salt
1/4 cup unsalted chicken stock

1/4 teaspoon ground cumin
1 tablespoon fresh cilantro
1 tablespoon honey
1/2 teaspoon fresh lime juice

Preheat the oven to 400 degrees F.

Layer the onion, garlic, and green tomatoes in a 9 x 13-inch glass baking dish. Sprinkle the salt over the vegetables. Add the chicken stock.

Bake the vegetables on the top rack of the oven for about 40 minutes, until soft and lightly browned.

Transfer the vegetables to a blender jar. Add the cumin, cilantro, honey, and lime juice. Blend until smooth. Season the sauce with additional salt to taste.

Serve warm or cold. Use immediately or store in an airtight container in the refrigerator for up to 1 week.

▶ *Makes about 2 1/4 cups.*

Roasted Grape Tomato Relish

The first time I experienced tomatoes as a sweet condiment was at Cotton Blues restaurant in Hattiesburg, Mississippi. The restaurant serves an appetizer of fried cheese curds with a tomato jam that is to die for. It made me rethink the ways I use tomatoes. After a trip to the farmers' market, I set out to create my own chunky tomato condiment. I ended up with what I call a tomato relish, equally delicious when used in appetizers and as a condiment for sandwiches or entrées. And for those of you like my mom, who enjoys ketchup with her beans, it adds a bright note. Try it with my Butter Bean Cassoulet (page 188).

2 pints small grape tomatoes

4 cloves garlic, minced

4 teaspoons finely diced red onion

4 teaspoons red wine vinegar

4 tablespoons pure cane sugar

1 teaspoon extra-virgin olive oil

1/4 teaspoon fine sea salt

1/4 teaspoon cracked black pepper

Pinch of cayenne pepper

Pinch of ground cinnamon

1/2 teaspoon chopped fresh oregano

1/2 teaspoon chopped fresh flat-leaf parsley

Preheat the oven to 400 degrees F.

Combine the grape tomatoes, garlic, onion, vinegar, sugar, oil, salt, black pepper, cayenne, and cinnamon on a baking sheet. Toss to coat and spread evenly in a single layer.

Bake for 8 minutes, then stir in the oregano and parsley. Bake for 8 to 9 more minutes, until the tomatoes are soft.

Transfer to a serving bowl or glass jar to serve, or store in an airtight container in the refrigerator for up to 1 week.

○ *Makes 2 cups.*

Roasted Barbecue Sauce

My great-grandmother Strahan never did anything in a small way, and my earliest memories of barbecue include her making a sweet and tangy homemade sauce by the gallon. My great-grandparents had a huge homemade brick barbecue pit, and on occasion, my great-grandmother would tell my dad that they needed to have a barbecue for his fellow coaches. This meant he had to undertake the huge endeavor of cutting wood for the pit and cooking more than twenty chickens. (The pit was that big!) With big shoes to fill and all those memories behind me, I was determined to make my own homemade barbecue sauce. Replacing the ketchup with fresh roasted tomatoes allowed me to lighten up the sauce and intensify the smoky flavor.

3 pounds vine-ripened tomatoes, sliced
1/2 red onion, sliced
4 cloves garlic, thinly sliced
1 cup firmly packed light brown sugar
1/2 cup pure cane sugar
2 cinnamon sticks

1/4 teaspoon fine sea salt
1/4 teaspoon cracked black pepper
1/3 cup red wine vinegar
1/2 chipotle pepper in adobo sauce, chopped
2 teaspoons soy sauce
1 teaspoon Worcestershire sauce

Preheat the oven to 400 degrees F.

Divide the tomato slices between two 9 x 13-inch glass baking dishes. Place half of the sliced onion and half of the garlic slices over the tomatoes in each pan. Divide the brown sugar, cane sugar, cinnamon sticks, salt, pepper, vinegar, chipotle pepper, soy sauce, and Worcestershire sauce between the two pans. Bake on the top rack of the oven for about 1 1/2 hours. Turn the pans around halfway through the baking time, and gently shake them to prevent the ingredients from sticking.

Working in batches, transfer the tomato mixture to a blender jar. Firmly secure the lid, place a kitchen towel on top, and hold down the lid while blending until smooth. Be careful while blending the hot liquid. Use immediately or store in jars in the refrigerator for up to 1 week.

◐ *Makes about 2 1/2 cups.*

Yogurt Aioli

This is my go-to dipping sauce and spread for everything from Smashed Potatoes (page 134) to Spiced Roasted Okra (page 141) to Breakfast Toast (page 24). This sauce is so addictive you will be dipping everything into it.

1/2 cup plain Greek yogurt
1/2 cup mayonnaise
1 clove garlic, minced

1 teaspoon finely grated lemon zest
1 teaspoon chopped fresh dill
Fine sea salt, to taste

Mix the yogurt, mayonnaise, garlic, lemon zest, and dill in a small bowl. Season the aioli with the salt to taste. Use immediately or store in an airtight container in the refrigerator for up to 1 week.

◗ *Makes about 1 cup.*

Sriracha Spread

Since being introduced to the Asian hot sauce Sriracha, I have tried to find fun and unexpected ways to include it in my Southern food repertoire. This spread is a spiced-up mayonnaise, but don't be afraid of the heat. When you try it on my Mississippi Banh Mi (page 111), you will become a fan too.

1 cup mayonnaise
2 tablespoons plus 2 teaspoons
    Sriracha hot chili sauce
4 teaspoons prepared horseradish

4 teaspoons Worcestershire sauce
4 teaspoons soy sauce
1/2 teaspoon fresh lime juice

Mix the mayonnaise, Sriracha, horseradish, Worcestershire sauce, soy sauce, and lime juice in a small bowl. Whisk until smooth. Use immediately or refrigerate for up to 1 week.

◗ *Makes about 1 cup.*

essentials and enhancers

Roasted Garlic

The mellow, sweet flavor of roasted garlic is nothing like the taste of sharp raw garlic. I make this recipe to use in many of my dishes, such as White Corn Soup (page 83), Pan-Seared Salmon with Persimmon Rum Sauce (page 220), Coconut Creamed Greens (page 147), and many more.

1 head garlic

1/4 teaspoon olive oil

Preheat the oven to 400 degrees F.

Remove the outer layers of the skin from the head of garlic and cut off about ¼ inch from the top, exposing the cloves. Place the garlic on a piece of aluminum foil. Drizzle the olive oil over the exposed cloves. Bring the edges of the aluminum foil together and crimp to close. Bake the garlic for 45 minutes to 1 hour, until fragrant and softened.

Fried Sage Leaves

This easy garnish is perfect for adding another layer of fall flavors to your recipes. Try it in my Roasted Butternut Squash Soup (page 86).

1 1/2 teaspoons extra-virgin olive oil

18 sage leaves

Heat the oil in a small sauté pan over medium-high heat. Add half of the sage leaves and cook for about 1 minute. Be careful because the oil may pop. Transfer to a paper towel to drain and crisp. Repeat with the remaining sage leaves.

Olive Oil Pie Dough

I believe that every bite of a pie should be delicious, and that includes the crust. This recipe makes that possible. It is simple to make and produces a deliciously flaky crust that holds up well under even the creamiest of fillings like my Turkey Potpie (page 190) and Mini Lemon Meringue Pies (page 261).

1/4 cup cold extra-virgin olive oil
1 1/2 cups all-purpose flour
1/4 teaspoon baking powder

1/4 teaspoon fine sea salt
2 teaspoons pure cane sugar
1/3 cup ice-cold water

Pour the olive oil in a small freezer-safe bowl. Freeze for 5 minutes. Do not freeze for any longer or it will harden.

Sift the flour, baking powder, and salt into a medium bowl. Stir in the sugar. Add the oil and mix with a fork until pea-size crumbs form.

Gradually add the cold water, stirring with a fork until the water is absorbed. Use your hands to lightly knead the dough and shape it into a ball.

Cover the dough with plastic wrap and refrigerate for about 30 minutes.

◉ *Makes 1 pie dough for a 9-inch piecrust.*

Homemade Caramel

With simple ingredients and easy-to-follow steps, my caramel recipe is a rich dip for green apples, but don't wait for Halloween. Try the Cracker Jack Panna Cotta (page 255) the next time you're hosting a dinner party, the Dessert Toast (page 233) the next time you want a little something sweet for brunch, or the Caramelized Banana Butter Pecan Cake (page 267) when you're celebrating a special occasion.

1 1/2 cups pure cane sugar

6 tablespoons unsalted butter, cubed and softened

1 cup heavy cream, room temperature

1/4 teaspoon fine sea salt

Sprinkle the sugar evenly over the bottom of a deep, heavy saucepan and heat over medium-high heat. Once the sugar begins to melt, swirl the pan to distribute the sugar evenly over the bottom of the pan. Do not stir. Once all of the sugar has melted, swirl the pan again.

Continue cooking until the sugar turns an amber color. If you are using an instant-read thermometer, cook the sugar until it reaches about 350 degrees F, being careful not to burn it. As soon as the caramel reaches this point, remove the pan from the heat, and add the butter all at once. Carefully whisk the butter into the bubbling caramel until incorporated. Slowly pour the cream into the bubbling caramel and whisk until smooth. Add the salt and whisk until incorporated.

Let the caramel cool for 10 minutes. Use immediately or refrigerate for up to 2 weeks.

● *Makes about 2 cups.*

Variations

For salted caramel, add 1 1/4 teaspoons flaky sea salt.

For vanilla caramel, add 1 teaspoon pure vanilla extract.

For sweet tea caramel, add 1 teaspoon strong brewed black tea.

Homemade Whipped Cream

The key to making the fluffiest whipped cream is to start with really cold cream and a cold bowl. Use 2 to 2½ tablespoons of powdered sugar, depending on how sweet you want the cream to be.

1 cup heavy cream, cold   2 to 2 ½ tablespoons powdered sugar

Place a large bowl in the freezer for 5 minutes. Remove the bowl from the freezer, pour in the heavy cream, and beat with an electric mixer on high speed until soft peaks form. Gradually beat in the powdered sugar. Use immediately or place in the refrigerator until serving time.

◗ *Makes about 2 cups.*

Acknowledgments

Sharing my love of hospitality and food through writing cookbooks continues to be a dream of mine, and I want to thank all of those people who have made it possible for me. Thank you, Mom, for the many hours you spent helping me prepare and test the recipes and lending me your prop-styling skills. Thank you, Dad, for your constant support, patience, taste testing, and dish washing. I love you. Thank you, Ryan, my husband, for your love and support and help with creating and taste testing the grilling and smoking recipes. Thank you, Brittyn and Leslie, my sisters, for your encouragement and support. Thank you, Chase and Scott, my brothers-in-law, for your taste testing. Thank you, John Michael and Emma Kate, my nephew and niece, for inspiring me to make my kid-friendly recipes.

I had a wonderful experience with my photo shoots in Memphis, Tennessee, at the Miller Barn in Lumberton, Mississippi, and at my parents' home in Poplarville, Mississippi. Thank you to my food photographer, Justin Fox Burks. You did a great job with the photography and props, making my food look its best. It was fun working with a fellow foodie. Thanks for making me feel at ease and for taking such natural photographs.

Thank you, Aunt Barbara and Uncle Jerry, for opening your home and letting me take over your kitchen for a week of cookbook photography. I hope the food made it somewhat worth it!

Thank you, WaWa, Nanny Ida, Aunt Diane, Drew, Mike, Kelli, Aunt Ilene,

Uncle Bill, Aunt Alene, Aunt Cora, Kirk, Teresa, Jennifer, Michael, Pop, Andrea, and Granny Christine, for your patience and support in trying all of my food experiments and participating in photo shoots.

Thank you, Kason, Trent, Gracie, Hayes, Hadley, Haden, DeAnna, Madison, Braden, and Kylea, for lending your appetites for sweets and participating in the photo shoots.

Thank you, PawPaw (Mike), Nanny (Margie), Mr. Terry, Mrs. Doreen, and Mr. Reed, for providing farm-fresh vegetables, fruits, fish, and meats for my recipe testing.

Thank you, Mrs. Alexander and the Poplarville Culinary Class, for all of your help in testing and preparing my recipes.

Thank you, David (Bubba) of The Little Butcher Shop, for your selection of meats used to create the recipes in this book.

Thank you, Etta B Pottery, for the beautiful pottery pieces that helped to make my food look good.

Thank you, Be Home. Your wood serving pieces are fantastic and were a great complement to my food picture backgrounds.

Thank you, California Olive Ranch, for your wonderful olive oil that I have found so many uses for in my recipes, from biscuits and pastry to all the savory dishes.

Thank you, Pam Lahaye of Apples Limited, for helping me stay well dressed for my photo shoots.

Thank you, Heather Skelton at Thomas Nelson, for all your assistance in putting together this cookbook. You have been a part of making my dream come true.

Last, but not least, I would like to thank all of my hometown taste testers: Mrs. Cynthia, Mrs. Glenda, Mrs. Debra, Mrs. Janet, and all of my friends, family, and acquaintances who have tasted my food and continue to inspire me to pursue my dream.

About the Author

Whitney Miller grew up in the small town of Poplarville, Mississippi, where her mother, grandmothers, and great-grandmothers taught her to cook at an early age. Her passion for cooking led her to the reality cooking show MasterChef in 2010, where at the age of twenty-two she became the first winner of the show. Soon afterward, she obtained a bachelor's degree-, with an emphasis in nutrition, from The University of Southern Mississippi.

Whitney's Southern cuisine has been enjoyed all over the United States and across the globe at her cooking events and demonstrations. She was the featured chef at Chefdance within the Sundance film festival in 2013 as well as at the St. Regis Tianjin in China for their Southern Food Promotion. She has shared her recipes and cooking tips through cooking demonstrations from New York City to Cape Town, South Africa.

Her career includes food writing and recipe development. Her recipes have been featured in *Flavors, Taste of Home, Southern Living, Clean Eating, Cooking Light, Southern Lady,* and *People* magazine.

Whitney uses her passion for cooking to help others, donating her speaking and cooking services to nonprofit organizations such as the Myasthenia Gravis Foundation of America, Tim Tebow Foundation, L.I.M.B.S International, and the Plant City Food Bank. She thanks Brian West with the Plant City Food

Bank for introducing her to her husband, Ryan Humphrey at the food bank's fundraising dinner last year.

Whitney lives in Plant City, Florida with her husband. Follow her on Twitter (@WhitneyMillerH) and Facebook (https://www.facebook.com/WhitneyMillerH) or visit her websitewww.whitneymiller.net to learn more about her speaking and cooking events.

Index

Index

305